where have all the
bluebirds gone?

where have all the bluebirds gone?

how to SOAR with FLEXIBLE GROUPING

JoAnne Schudt Caldwell & Michael P. Ford

HEINEMANN
Portsmouth, NH

Heinemann
A division of Reed Elsevier Inc.
361 Hanover Street
Portsmouth, NH 03801–3912
www.heinemann.com

Offices and agents throughout the world

The authors and publisher wish to thank those who have generously given permission to reprint borrowed material:

"Membership Card for Wee Readers Club" and "Wee Readers Punch Card" are adapted by permission of Gloria Harter, Oshkosh Area School District, Oshkosh, Wisconsin.

"The Reading Workshop" is adapted from "Organizing for Effective Instruction: The Reading Workshop" by Ray Reutzel and Robert Cooter, Jr. in *The Reading Teacher* 44(8). Copyright © 1991 by the International Reading Association. All rights reserved.

Library of Congress Cataloging-in-Publication Data
Caldwell, JoAnne.
    Where have all the bluebirds gone? : how to soar with flexible grouping / JoAnne Schudt Caldwell, Michael P. Ford.
        p.   cm.
    Includes bibliographical references.
    ISBN 0-325-00437-4 (pbk. : alk. paper)
    1. Reading.   2. Mixed ability grouping in education.   3. Group reading.   I. Ford, Michael P.   II. Title.

LB1050 .C215   2002
372.41′62—dc21   2002006314

Editor: Lois Bridges
Production: Lynne Reed
Cover design: Jenny Jensen Greenleaf
Typesetter: TechBooks
Manufacturing: Steve Bernier

Printed in the United States of America on acid-free paper
09   08   07   06   VP   7   8   9   10

To teachers
Those who have influenced us
Those with whom we have worked
And those we are preparing for the future
And
To those students who will benefit the most
from the insights and ideas in this book

JSC & MPF

Contents

Acknowledgments

WE NEED TO ACKNOWLEDGE THE ROLE THAT THE WISCONSIN State Reading Association (WSRA) has played in supporting the work that has evolved into this book. The Wisconsin State Reading Association has always recognized its leadership role in improving reading instruction within and beyond its state boundaries. In 1991, WSRA President Lorraine Gerhart approached Dr. JoAnne Caldwell of Cardinal Stritch University to chair an ad hoc committee. The committee was charged with the task of examining grouping practices in reading programs and developing a position statement that educators could use to support changes in the practice of ability grouping. Dr. Caldwell was joined by Dr. Michael Ford of the University of Wisconsin Oshkosh. They worked with committee members Leslie Balliet, Beverly Bell, Jacqueline Karbon, Jeanne Olsheske, Barbara Sands, Suzanne Terry, Claudia Whitty, and Gloria Weiner. They began a serious exploration of two key issues: (1) the research on ability grouping, and (2) classroom alternatives to traditional grouping practices. The authors want to acknowledge the work of those initial committee members, which forms a foundation for this book.

The group developed a position statement that was approved by the WSRA Executive Committee and was presented to the membership. The committee felt, however, that the position statement alone might not be enough to support change away from ability grouping. The committee decided to develop a more complete resource to provide insights and ideas that might assist educators in learning about and experimenting with different grouping practices. A monograph was the result of those efforts, and this book is an updated, revised version of that work. The authors want to acknowledge specifically contributors to the original monograph who shared their voices as researchers and classroom teachers: Jeanne Olsheske, Barbara Sands, Beverly

Bell, Jacqueline Karbon, Suzanne Terry, Gloria Harter, Brenda Wallace, Marcia Winship, Mary Rae Johnson, and Paola Wegner. We hope that we have captured the essence of their insights and ideas in building on those contributions for this book.

The authors would also like to express their appreciation to Sandra Wilde for bringing this work to the attention of Heinemann editor Lois Bridges, and to Lois for her continuous support of this work.

Introduction

A View from the Past: A Vision of the Future

About forty years ago, many American families watched a popular sitcom on television, *Leave It to Beaver*. Each week, young Beaver or his older brother, Wally, would encounter some sort of problem. This was neatly solved in thirty minutes, usually due to the wise suggestions of Beaver's parents: his mother, who wore high heels and pearls to fix breakfast, and his father, who wore three-piece suits while he read the newspaper before dinner. Occasionally, the show visited Beaver's classroom, which was presided over by his teacher, Miss Landers. Beaver and his classmates sat at desks that were lined up in perfect rows. They raised their hands when they wanted to talk, and they stood by the side of their desks when they did so. Of course, Miss Landers' classroom was fiction, but it is not difficult to imagine what might have occurred during Beaver's reading instruction.

Beaver's classmates were divided into three reading groups: the high, the middle, and the low. In the past each reading group had a name: the Sparrows, the Bluebirds, and the Cardinals. These names fooled no one. Group members all knew the exact status of their group. Beaver, a television writer's embodiment of the average boy, was probably in the middle group. At the start of the reading lesson, Miss Landers handed out worksheets to keep the students occupied while she worked with each reading group. She encouraged them to work independently, quietly, and industriously. Then Miss Landers called Beaver's group to come to the front of the room. The group settled themselves in chairs arranged in a circle, each member clutching his or her basal reader and workbook. Miss Landers chose a basal selection and asked each child to read a page aloud. Although Beaver read well, he was worried. Last week, he was quite embarrassed when he stumbled on a word and a group member called out the correct pronunciation. In order to prevent this from happening again, our intrepid hero figured out which page would come up for his reading turn, and he surreptitiously practiced it while the other group members were reading. After a bout of round robin reading, Miss Landers asked the children to open their workbooks. She gave instructions on a specific skill and helped them begin the assigned pages. Then they returned to their seats to finish the workbook pages and attack the worksheets while Miss Landers called up the next two groups.

Once a week, Miss Landers took her class to the school library, where they were allowed to choose books to read on their own. They kept these books in their desks to read when they finished their worksheets. Of course, many children never finished their worksheets, so they never read much and simply exchanged one unread book for another during these library visits. Miss Landers used book reports as a way of checking on the students' outside reading. Those children who seldom finished a book were very creative in borrowing book reports from their peers or inventing generic reports on books they never read.

Of course, Miss Landers also taught writing. Beaver and his classmates worked doggedly through worksheets on commas, capital letters, and sentence fragments. Once a week, Miss Landers assigned a composition to the class. Everyone wrote on the same topic, such as "My Best Friend" or "My Trip to the Zoo." The children wrote by themselves, sometimes in class and often for homework. Miss Landers collected the papers, corrected them with red pencil, and graded them. Occasionally, a student might read his or her composition to the class, but more often Miss Landers handed back the corrected papers and hung a few sterling examples on the bulletin board.

Beaver and his friends were motivated students. They did what they were told even if totally bored, and if they misbehaved, a combination of principal and parent input solved any problems in thirty minutes.

A Vision of the Future

Fast forward forty years. What would Miss Landers' classroom look like now? Our purpose in this book is to create a vision of classroom reading programs far different from that view of the past. Imagine a classroom in which space has been reorganized to allow students to work in large-group settings and come together to work in small groups or teams. Imagine a classroom where students can find special spaces to work with a partner or work independently on their own.

Imagine a classroom in which a student's group assignment does not define who the student is. Through a combination of large groups, small groups, teams, and partners, students contribute to a variety of situations. Some of the time, students might be working with peers who are more alike in their achievement levels or skill needs. At other times, students might be working with peers of mixed abilities and talents, so that everyone can make a contribution to the activity at hand. And even when students know they are struggling, they do not have to endure classroom structures that serve as daily reminders to them (and everyone else) of their low status.

> **Through a combination of large groups, small groups, teams, and partners, students contribute to a variety of situations.**

Imagine small-group work with the teacher that is planned on the basis of the readers' needs and the expectations of the school. It is not directed by what a commercial publisher suggests or based on suggestions in a teacher's manual. The small-group work can be focused around many types of texts, including basal selections, trade books, and magazines. These materials are read by the students in many creative ways without relying on a round robin style. The students can actually listen to one another and engage in a variety of response activities to deepen their understandings and extend their connections.

Imagine independent work that students are engaged in away from the teacher—independent work that rivals the power of the teacher's instruction. Imagine authentic activities replacing the huge stacks of workbook pages and worksheets. Students read and write away from the teacher. Classroom structures such as centers or learning stations keep students independently engaged in working with print when they are not meeting with the teacher. Classroom structures allow students to meet together to read, discuss, and respond to stories. Independent structures promote inquiry-based investigations and allow partners and individuals to work on projects using reading and writing to learn about critical issues and answer questions.

Imagine small-group reading instruction that is placed within an overall flexible grouping plan. Imagine grouping that provides students with large-group activities to build community through shared experiences, as well as moments for individual activities where students can read and respond to self-selected books and texts. Imagine reading instruction that is fully integrated with writing instruction, with one flowing out of and into the other. Imagine a focus not only on writing mechanics but also on the processes of reading and writing.

What might Beaver and his friends say about Miss Landers' classroom now? Her classroom reading program has been influenced by the insights, issues, and ideas that the field has gained about grouping practices since the time Beaver graduated from elementary school. Miss Landers' classroom now provides a flexible arrangement of grouping experiences for students, an arrangement that is driven by the professional decision making of the classroom teacher. It is based on the needs of the students and considerate of the expectations of the school. We believe that the possibility of such a reading program should be the vision that helps all of us transform ability-based classroom reading programs into a new model of how students are grouped in reading programs. This book, which begins with a question-and-answer format and concludes with real classroom examples, can show teachers how.

where have all the
bluebirds gone?

1

Grouping Patterns in
Reading Instruction

What Research Tells Us

TODAY'S CLASSROOMS ARE EXTREMELY DIVERSE. CHILDREN COME from a variety of home environments and family structures. Many of these are supportive; some are not. Children enter our classrooms with a multitude of personal and educational needs. English is the first language for some children, but many speak a different language. Some can read grade-level text; others cannot. Some children are motivated to read; others have little use for literacy activities. Our students may also bear a variety of labels, such as learning disabled, emotionally disturbed, ADHD, cognitively disabled, and more. Teachers struggle daily to handle this complexity. The common instructional practice of organizing students into different groups can be an effective instructional tool for meeting their diverse needs.

What Forms of Classroom Grouping Are Most Common for Reading Instruction?

The most common form of classroom grouping in elementary reading instruction has been ability grouping (Haskins, Walden, and Ramey, 1983; Sorenson and Hallinan, 1986; Barr and Dreeben, 1991; Palardy, 1991; Nagel, 2000). In 1988, data from the National Assessment of Educational Progress (NAEP) showed that 80 percent of students in fourth grade were in reading groups formed on the basis of ability (Langer, Applebee, Mullis, and Foertsch, 1990). To facilitate teaching and learning, educators sort children into separate classrooms (between-class grouping) or separate groups within a classroom (within-class grouping) according to their perceived reading ability

(Hallinan, 1984). Unfortunately, in many classrooms, this is the only form of grouping used in reading instruction (Barr and Dreeben, 1991). These group assignments tend to become fixed, and many children remain in the same level of grouping throughout their elementary years (Hiebert, 1983; Johnston and Markle, 1983; Goodlad, 1984; Gamoran, 1989, 1991).

> **Group assignments tend to become fixed, and many children remain in the same level of grouping throughout their elementary years.**

Ability grouping is also the principal mode of grouping for children who need some form of reading intervention (Allington and McGill-Franzen, 1989a, 1989b). Middle and secondary schools are dominated by another form of ability grouping, called tracking (Slavin, 1990). Educators sort students into different ability levels, often for all of their content area classes.

A second dominant and common form of classroom grouping is whole-class grouping (Nagel, 2000). Most content area instruction in both elementary and secondary schools is directed to the class as a whole. Some defend whole-class instruction as offering the same learning opportunities to all students and as "emphasizing the open, democratic principles of the educational system and the realities of life in a 'survival of the fittest world'" (Lou, Abrami, and Spence, 2000, p. 101).

Whole-class grouping is growing in popularity in elementary reading classrooms, perhaps as a reaction to the dominance of ability grouping and its perceived drawbacks (Reutzel and Cooter, 1996). When Moody, Vaughn, and Schumm (1997) interviewed both general and special educators, general educators revealed a move away from ability grouping. Many employed both whole-class grouping and mixed-ability small groups, first instructing the class as a whole and then using smaller mixed groupings for practice and reinforcement.

What Criteria Do Educators Use for Placing Students in These Groups?

There are no special criteria for whole-group placement; students are part of the group by virtue of their assignment to the classroom. However the term "ability group" suggests that teachers form groups on the basis of reading ability. Other factors may also play prominent roles (Strike, 1983; Haller and Waterman, 1985). Teachers often place children in groups on the basis of behavior and personality characteristics, work habits, achievement in other subjects, and home environment. For the higher groups, teachers tend to select children perceived as respectful toward authority, children who interact well with their peers, and children who display good work habits. On the other hand, teachers tend to place in the lower groups children who are seen as immature, lacking in motivation, somewhat noisy, and sometimes confrontive (Eder, 1981; Borko, 1982; Good and Marshall, 1984; Hallinan, 1984). Because of the varied factors that can influence placement in reading groups, it may be misleading to use the term "ability" (Strike, 1983; Nagel, 2000).

Group placement can also depend upon factors such as class size and the number of books available for each group (Dreeben, 1984; Barr, 1975). Parents also play a role by actively intervening in decisions regarding group placement and by forcefully questioning placements not to their liking (Gamoran, 1991). As well, the previous year's teacher and district policy often dictate group placement. Some districts or principals frown upon groups that are made up of all boys or all girls or of groups that are predominantly made up of students of one race. Different teachers in the same school or district may form groups on the basis of different criteria, and different teachers may attach different levels of importance to the criteria they use.

At the middle school and secondary levels, educators commonly use standardized achievement tests to assign students to tracks. Unfortunately, large differences on these test scores do not necessarily equate to similar large differences in what students actually know or can learn (Oakes, 1985). Intelligence test scores also determine tracking assignments, but many criticize such measures as testing only a narrow range of abilities and reflecting just present knowledge, not future potential (Riccio, 1985). Teacher or counselor judgment represents another factor in tracking decisions, but such judgment may be extremely subjective and based on factors other than ability (Riccio, 1985).

What Type of Interaction and Instruction Is Common in Ability Groups and Whole-Class Groupings?

Interaction

Group interaction and teacher instruction tends to differ between different ability group levels. In low-ability reading groups, the need to maintain discipline and to control inappropriate behavior often works against effective instructional practices (Eder, 1981; Johnston and Markle, 1983). In such groups, members are more inattentive than their higher-placed peers, and teachers tolerate greater inattention (Gambrell, Wilson, and Ganatt, 1981; Eder 1981;

Allington, 1983a). As well, "peer influence in low-ability groups tends to be unavoidable and strong enough to overwhelm the potential instructional advantages of grouping" (Good and Marshall, 1984, p. 22). As a result, students who seem to experience the most difficulty are often members of groups whose social contexts are not conducive to learning (Eder, 1981).

Instruction

Members of reading ability groups do not just read different selections. In many cases, they also receive different forms of instruction, with the interaction between teacher and group members differing for each group. Usually, instruction for children in the high groups centers on meaningful discussion of stories (Alpert, 1975). They discuss why a character acted in a certain way, how a story reminded them of their own experiences, or what they learned about a new topic. In contrast, children in the low groups tend to receive instruction centered on identifying words and sounds (Allington, 1983a; Hiebert, 1983; Allington and McGill-Franzen, 1989a).

Teachers evaluate good readers on their answers to questions about the selection. They often judge poor readers on their ability to say a word correctly (Allington and McGill-Franzen, 1989a). When children mispronounce a word, teachers interrupt more often in low reading groups (Allington, 1980; Pflaum, Pascarella, Boswick, and Auer, 1980; Allington, 1983a; Haskins, Walden, and Ramey, 1983). They provide letter and sound clues to low groups and meaning cues to high groups.

Ability groups also differ in the amount and kind of reading that children do. Good readers read almost three times as many words per day as poor readers. Poor readers do more oral reading, while good readers spend 70 percent of their time reading silently (Allington, 1980, 1983a, 1984).

At the secondary level, teachers provide structural clues to answers for low-track students but ask high-track students to evaluate the evidence provided in the text (French and Rothman, 1990). Low-track students receive diluted class content and move at a slower pace than their high-track peers. They are "not expected to synthesize material or apply content to problem situations and their curriculum often takes 'a recipe approach' based upon instruction in component skills" (French and Rothman, 1990, p. 5). Oakes (1988) suggests that teachers of low tracks emphasize discipline and behavior more than learning and tend to be "less encouraging and more punitive" (p. 43). Gamoran, Nystrand, Berends, and LePore (1995) compared homogeneous classes at different ability levels in twenty-five secondary schools. They found consistently more off-task behavior in the remedial tracks.

A somewhat different pattern emerges for whole-class grouping: "In whole class instruction, there is often an emphasis on the uniformity, rather than the diversity, of instruction" (Lou, Abrami, and Spence, 2000). As well, whole-class instruction has been dominated by a transmission approach to learning (Wade and Moje, 2000). The teacher is in control and chooses the knowledge or skills to be transmitted and the text to be read or listened to. The students are expected to pay attention, follow directions, respond appropriately, and document their learning in some way. The emphasis is on "teacher explanations and encouragement, rather than on peer explanations and encouragement, to promote student learning" (Lou, Abrami, and Spence, 2000). In content classrooms, the same subject area text is given to all students irrespective of their reading ability (Alvermann and Moore, 1991). Because students often cannot read the text, teachers often choose a lecture or demonstration format to transmit information (Wade and Moje, 2000). Disadvantages to whole-class instruction include less attention to individual needs, less pupil-to-pupil interaction, less opportunity for "kidwatching," and less opportunity for some students to participate (Radencich, McKay, and Paratore, 1995).

> **Whole-class instruction has been dominated by a transmission approach to learning.**

How Are Students Affected by Grouping?

Perhaps the most problematic effect of whole-class grouping is its inability to meet the needs of individual children (Reutzel, 1999). Children often cannot read the assigned text, which limits their ability to actively participate in the discussion and complete class activities. As well, many children become "lost" in whole-group instruction; they sit quietly and rarely interact with their peers. Others relieve their frustration by acting out, often inappropriately.

Perhaps the most insidious effect of ability grouping is the stigma attached to placement in the low group. Children are aware of group placement despite teacher efforts to disguise the group status (Filby, Barnett, and Bossert, 1982; Eder, 1981). Group placement affects how they feel about themselves as students and as readers (Weinstein, 1976; Good and Marshall, 1984; George, 1988).

The social status of students in high and low groups differs (Hallinan, 1984). Both students and teachers perceive high-group members more positively. Ability grouping also affects social interactions. Students tend to stay with their group on the playground, in the lunch room, and during ungrouped class activities. In this way, the group or track limits friendship choices (Sorenson and Hallinan, 1986).

Another effect of placement into high and low groups is the creation of different expectations for achievement on the part of both pupils and teachers (Good and Brophy, 1987; Good and Marshall, 1984). As noted, teachers make fewer demands on low-group students and set less exacting standards (Oakes, 1985). Low expectations often result in "a self-fulfilling prophecy of low-performing students, thereby contributing to a cycle of failure and lowered academic achievement and motivation" (French and Rothman, 1990, p. 4).

Another negative effect of ability grouping is the fact that children seldom move out of groups. Although there is some movement in and out of placements in the first two grades or in the first month of the academic year, reading group assignment in first grade largely determines assignment in second grade (Juel, 1990). By third or fourth grade, group assignments are relatively fixed (Barr and Dreeben, 1988; Goodlad, 1984).

Does Ability Grouping Work? Does Whole-Class Grouping Work?

These are not simple questions to answer. Gamoran (1987) points out that "grouping does not produce achievement; instruction does" (p. 341). Achievement differences may be due to variation in instruction, not to the grouping itself (Esposito, 1973; Kulik and Kulik, 1982; Hiebert, 1983; Rowan and Miracle, 1983; Young and McCullough, 1992; Barr, 1995).

Grouping does not produce achievement; instruction does.

Researchers have examined the effectiveness of ability grouping by comparing ability-grouped classes to heterogeneously grouped control classes. Such comparisons have yielded mixed results. Slavin (1987) reviewed several types of elementary ability grouping. He examined effects for between-class grouping—that is, assigning students to one self-contained class on the basis of ability or achievement. Slavin concluded that "research evidence refutes the assertion that ability-grouped class assignment can increase student achievement" (p. 307).

If students are not assigned to a self-contained class on the basis of achievement, they are generally regrouped for reading instruction. Some leave their heterogeneous classrooms and receive instruction separately with peers of similar achievement. Others receive instruction in small reading groups within their classroom (within-class grouping). Few studies have examined the effectiveness of either form of regrouping, and results are inconclusive (Slavin, 1987). Some evidence exists for positive effects on reading achievement for students who participate in the Joplin Plan (Slavin, 1987). In this plan, students are regrouped by reading level across grade-level lines. That is, all students reading at a third-grade level are instructed together regardless of their chronological grade level. Slavin (1990) also reviewed grouping in secondary schools and concluded that "the effects of ability grouping on student achievement are essentially zero" (p. 484).

Other researchers also suggest that ability groups do not necessarily enhance achievement and may, in fact, widen the gap between the low and high groups (Esposito, 1973; Kulik and Kulik, 1982; Hiebert, 1983; Johnston and Markle, 1983; Good and Marshall, 1984). Gamoran, Nystrand, Berends, and LePore (1995) found that off-task behavior and incomplete work were more detrimental to achievement in remedial groups than to achievement in honors groups. While students in high groups do achieve more than their lower-placed peers, ability grouping has only a small effect on low or average learners (Kulik and Kulik, 1982; Riccio, 1985). Some researchers suggest that traditional grouping practices are deterrents to learning for students assigned to the low groups. The slight effect of ability grouping in helping high achievers is "offset by substantial losses by the average and low groups" (Hallinan, 1984, p. 232).

Jones and Gerig (1994) examined the frequency and quality of sixth-grade student interactions in homogeneous and heterogeneous classes. They found that low achievers and African American students tended to interact more in ability-grouped settings. High achievers interacted more in mixed-ability classes. The researchers found little differences in the quality of interactions across either group.

What do students think about grouping? Jones and Gerig (1994) interviewed sixth graders who were ability grouped for language arts and mathematics and heterogeneously grouped for social studies and science. Low achievers favored heterogeneous groupings because they enjoyed the challenge and the opportunity to learn from their peers. High-ability students preferred to be grouped with peers of similar ability because they liked the faster pace of the class and the fact that they were less bored.

Similarly, Elbaum, Moody, and Schumm (1999) administered a questionnaire to third-through fifth-grade students and asked them to rate different grouping patterns: whole-class, mixed-ability groups, same-ability groups, mixed-ability pairs, same-ability pairs, and independent work. Students rated mixed-ability groups and mixed-ability pairs the highest. They assigned lowest ratings to same-ability groups and independent work. Following the question- naire, the researchers interviewed a subset of students and identified some in- teresting patterns. Students with and without a learning disability commented on the noise and distractions that are often present when the class is divided into small groups. They mentioned that it was difficult to obtain teacher help when the class was so divided. Students of lower ability also expressed concern about being embarrassed in mixed-ability groups. Higher-ability students in- dicated a preference for working with peers of similar ability because they could maintain a faster pace of learning.

It is interesting that little research has investigated the effectiveness of whole-class grouping as compared to other forms of grouping. Lou, Abrami, Spence, Poulsen, Chambers, and d'Apollonia (1996) reviewed studies that compared classrooms that used homogeneous and heterogeneous small groups to whole-class formats that did not employ grouping. They found a significant achievement effect for small groups. However, student achievement was clearly influenced by factors other than grouping: differentiated instruc- tion, the kinds of materials used, the number and kind of reward strategies employed, and teacher training and experience. Students of all ability levels benefitted from learning in small groups, but lower-ability students achieved more. Further, lower-ability students learned more in heterogeneous small groups, while medium-ability students learned more in homogeneous small groups. Group composition made little difference in the achievement of high- ability students, and overall, student achievement varied with regard to subject area. In particular, small groups seemed more effective for math and science as opposed to reading and language arts.

In summary, research has not demonstrated the overall efficacy of ability grouping and has not documented the effectiveness of whole-class grouping. Perhaps this is because many variables other than grouping play a part in fostering student achievement. However, re- search does offer some cautions to the reading

Teachers should employ a flexible grouping format designed to meet new needs as they arise.

teacher. There are negative aspects to both abil- ity grouping and to whole-class grouping. For this reason, the teacher should examine other grouping patterns, such as literature circles, co- operative learning groups, and guided reading groups (Reutzel, 1999). Teachers should avoid reliance upon one grouping pattern to the exclusion of others and instead employ a flexible grouping format where group membership is not fixed and where groups are "periodically created, modified, or disbanded to meet new needs as they arise" (Reutzel, 1999, p. 276).

When Should Educators Use Ability Grouping for Reading Instruction?

Ability grouping can work under certain conditions (Slavin, 1987). First, an effective ability group reflects a narrow band of ability—that is, teachers choose group members because of very specific needs. This might involve a group of children who are experiencing difficulty summarizing a story or a group that needs to practice reading fluently. Such needs are more specifically defined than the broad category of reading ability. Second, the teacher designs the instruction to carefully match the needs of the group. In this example, instruction centers on summarization or fluency activities and nothing else. Third, the teacher frequently assesses and changes group membership. As children demonstrate improvement in summarizing stories or reading fluently, the teacher disbands the group and forms new ones.

Instead of referring to these groups as "ability groups," Reutzel suggests calling them "needs groupings": "The purpose of a needs group is to teach a temporary group of students a particular procedure, literary stylistic device, skill, or strategy they have yet to learn and apply" (1999, p. 281). Needs grouping is the result of careful teacher assessment and observation that identifies several students with similar instructional needs.

What About Guided Reading? Isn't This a Form of Ability Grouping?

One of the most popular uses of small groups is for guided reading (Fountas and Pinnell, 1996). Guided reading does look very much like ability grouping in that students are grouped according to their ability to read leveled books (Reutzel, 1999; Brown, 1999–2000). In fact, in their view of New Zealand literacy programs, Wilkinson and Townsend (2000) suggest that guided reading provides a more positive view of ability grouping. However, initial group formation and later regrouping is not based upon a general estimation of reading ability but upon a student's ability to read successfully a book that represents a specific level of difficulty. Guided reading groups are the context for systematically teaching children how to unlock meaning as they read.

At the same time, if guided reading is the only grouping pattern used in a classroom, it can exhibit all the negative aspects traditionally associated with ability grouping (Opitz and Ford, 2001). As Reutzel (1999) notes,

"Children should not be placed in guided reading groups until they have had ample opportunities to listen to stories, poems, songs, etc. and to participate in shared and community-based whole class reading experiences" (p. 284). Guided reading should never represent the sum total of a child's classroom reading instruction. Only when these groups are integrated within the total language arts program can they provide an effective form of instruction for all readers (Wilkinson and Townsend, 2000).

> **Guided reading should never represent the sum total of a child's classroom reading instruction.**

What Directions Should Educators Take with Regard to Grouping Patterns?

Unfortunately, educators have tended to rely upon a single form of classroom grouping. This has not acted in the best interests of students. According to Hallinan, "The effects of instructional grouping as practiced in United States schools today are not consistent with the educational goals of maximizing student intellectual potential and creating equal opportunities for educational achievement" (Hallinan, 1984, pp. 238–239). If this is true, and many educators believe it is, then we have no choice but to examine our grouping practices at both the elementary and secondary levels. We must experiment with different grouping formats, such as interest grouping, cooperative grouping, and peer tutoring. We must form temporary needs groupings when indicated. We must provide regular opportunities for students to interact in multiability groups. We must hold high expectations for all, treat each student as a learner capable of achieving, and make the acquisition of higher-order thinking skills a priority for all students (Michigan Reading Association, 1991). We must continually examine our instruction, our expectations, and patterns of student interaction to ensure that all learners receive meaningful instruction in whatever grouping format we choose.

Why Should Educators Consider Different Grouping Formats?

It is important that we help students develop comfortable relationships with other students and with persons of authority. Students who do not feel isolated, rejected, or disconnected from others will be better learners. They will be able to contribute more to their present academic lives. Students who listen to one another and accept one another have a better chance of finding success in a global and multicultural future. When educators rigidly emphasize one form of grouping pattern, either ability grouping or whole-class grouping, positive relationships between students are less developed than if a variety of grouping formats are followed.

What Is an Effective Grouping Pattern?

Effective groups are groups that enhance student learning. The teacher determines the most appropriate grouping pattern for each instructional experience by carefully analyzing the purpose of the instruction and students' strengths and needs. The teacher then matches this information with the grouping choices available.

Effective groups are flexible, which means that the teacher uses different grouping patterns for different purposes and at different times during the school year. In flexible grouping, the teacher places students in temporary groups. The groups remain in place until the purpose of instruction has been achieved. Then the teacher disbands the groups and forms new ones. Flexible grouping is based on the premise that every instructional lesson demands careful attention by the teacher in matching students' needs with the most appropriate grouping format.

Effective grouping patterns encourage interactions between students as well as interactions between the teacher and students. Using a flexible approach to grouping ensures that the best grouping patterns will be used when most appropriate. Flexible grouping provides an exciting alternative to rigid adherence to ability grouping or whole-class grouping as the single grouping format.

Flexible grouping provides an exciting alternative to ability grouping or whole-class grouping.

How Many Kinds of Grouping Are There?

There are many ways to group students. Groups may vary in terms of their purpose, their activity, their membership, their size, and the materials they work with. The whole class can form a group, with members discussing a selection that all have read or working on a skill that all need. Students can work in cooperative groups to achieve a common purpose or produce a common product for which they receive a group grade. Students can collaborate in small groups to share their thoughts and opinions about a selection or to prepare for individual evaluation. Students can form interest groups to pursue a topic of concern or read a book of their choice. The teacher can place students in temporary skill groups to address a specific need, such as decoding or punctuation. Students can work as buddies or partners to orally read selections for improvement of fluency. Students can work individually to independently practice what has been learned in other groups. No matter what type of grouping the teacher uses, the task must be clear and appropriate to the needs and interests of the students involved.

What Are Some Benefits of Flexible Grouping?

In the process of working with small groups of learners who function well together in a variety of situations, students not only learn content but they acquire interpersonal and small-group skills. They become more independent learners. They become individually accountable for working alone or in a group. They develop skills in face-to-face interaction. Students learn to work in groups with a noise level that does not detract from the work of others, and they learn to move about the room without causing disruption.

Flexible grouping also has benefits for the teacher. The teacher can fit grouping patterns to the needs of the students. Flexible grouping allows for more creativity on the part of the teacher. Classroom arrangements are not static but change according to the demands of the instruction focus.

What Should a Teacher Keep in Mind
When Selecting a Grouping Pattern?

Each grouping pattern has advantages and disadvantages, and each works well under some conditions but fails under others. The chart provided in the appendix presents an overview of common grouping patterns in hopes of assisting teachers to best match students' needs with the most appropriate group experience. The patterns presented in the chart are discussed at length in the chapters that follow.

2

Whole-Group Instruction
One Text for All Readers

What Is Whole-Group Instruction?

Whole-group instruction occurs when everyone in the class reads the same text. They may read the same basal reader selection, the same trade book, or the same content area textbook. Whole-group instruction also occurs when everyone listens to the same lecture, watches the same video, performs the same task, or practices the same skill.

Can Whole-Group Instruction Be an Effective Format for Reading Instruction?

Teachers often use a single selection in elementary content area instruction. That is, one science, social studies, or math textbook serves the entire class. Similarly, having all students read the same story or expository selection can be an effective part of reading instruction. For example, the teacher could use a single selection to model strategic reading to the entire class. Lessons might focus on the importance of self-questioning or how to summarize. In some cases, teachers may choose a single text because the school curriculum directs that all students in a certain grade read a specific trade book. As well, limited materials may dictate frequent use of one selection for the entire class.

> **Involving the whole class in a single selection can motivate readers.**

Involving the whole class in a single selection can be very motivating for readers, who see themselves as participating members of an entire class, not an ability group. The class can enjoy poems from different cultures or read selections about topics of common interest. There is, however, a serious disadvantage to having all students read the same text. Some may not be able to handle it successfully. They may not be able to read the words and, as a result, their comprehension suffers. Such students withdraw from the class activity, either quietly or with disruptive behaviors. As well, their inability to keep up with their peers often reinforces their negative perceptions of themselves as readers and as students. Fortunately, a teacher can overcome this disadvantage by following a simple practice: Avoid any independent reading of the text by students who cannot successfully handle it. The next section suggests ways to handle this issue.

> **Avoid any independent reading of the text by students who cannot successfully handle it. Instead, use other methods to support their reading and comprehension.**

What Different Reading Formats Can Be Used with Whole-Group Instruction?

Many people think there are only two ways for students to read a selection: (1) silently and independently or (2) orally, in turns. Neither way protects students who cannot successfully handle the selection. If directed to read silently, these students may merely turn pages and let their eyes run passively over the text. If asked to read orally, students may be embarrassed in front of peers by a stumbling, halting performance full of errors. There are, however, a variety of other ways for students to read a selection. Let us address oral reading first.

Oral Reading

Shared reading (also called choral reading) is one form of oral reading. It is based on the assumption that students will benefit from reading a selection with peers who can supply the pronunciation of unknown words. Thus, decoding ability does not limit a student's participation in shared reading. The teacher and students read orally together in unison. The teacher models expressive oral reading, sets a fluent pace, and does not slow down to match the students' pace. (The students will always be slightly behind the teacher.)

All students benefit from teacher modeling of good oral reading behaviors and from hearing unknown words pronounced correctly. In addition, shared reading is very nonthreatening to the less able readers, who do not need to read every word aloud. As an alternative to shared reading, the teacher can read some parts with the students and have the students chorally read other sections without the teacher. In this format, the better readers in the class take the lead and play the teacher's part.

Another form of oral reading that avoids individual independent reading is partner reading. Students can read orally together in partners or triads. According to Stahl and Heubach (1993), there were no difficulties when students chose their own partners. Students should be allowed to choose their own partners. Students prefer to read with friends, even if there is a difference in reading levels. Partner reading also encourages them to help each other figure out unknown words.

Silent Reading

What different forms of silent reading can a teacher use? The teacher can read to the students while they silently follow along in their book. In this way, they see unknown words as they hear the teacher say them. Students can also silently read a selection while listening to a tape. Again, the key is for the students to follow along and not merely listen. Many students can reread a selection on their own if they have heard it first and if they have tracked the text as they listened.

Often, readers struggling the most in a class cannot even follow the words. These students can benefit from just listening to the selection. Resource personnel or parents can read the selection to them or they can listen to a tape. In this way, students gain knowledge of text content through listening, and they can participate in class discussions and activities.

Partners can read together silently as well as orally. The partners take turns being the lead reader. The lead reader sets the pace. When the lead reader finishes a page, the partner must stop reading, even if not finished. The lead partner then retells what has been read. The other partner adds to this retelling, verifies it, or corrects it. Then the partners switch roles.

In independent silent reading, the whole class reads the same selection, but each student reads at an individual pace. This only works if all students in the class are adequately able to decode and comprehend the material on their own. Again, this is seldom the case. Some students may find the assigned text extremely easy, perhaps even unchallenging. Others may find it so difficult as to be frustrating. If independent silent reading of a single selection is to work, the teacher will have to find ways to accommodate a variety of reading levels within the class. For example, parents, aides, or older students can read to and with individuals who cannot handle the text independently. Alternately, the teacher can ask able students to read the selection independently while the teacher guides the less able students through it. However, Paratore (1990) cautions that this can prove dangerous. If a teacher does this on a regular basis and if the group is always composed of the same students, it then becomes an ability group.

How Can a Teacher Manipulate These Various Formats of Reading in Whole-Group Instruction?

Much depends upon the length and type of the selection. Most selections for upper-elementary students are too long for teachers to rely totally upon one form of reading. However, a teacher can divide any selection to include a variety of reading formats and gradually release the responsibility to the readers (Pearson and Gallagher, 1983). For example, the first part of a selection is often the most difficult as the author introduces topic, purpose, and characters. The teacher may begin by reading to the students while they follow along. The teacher can then move into shared reading, alternating between reading with the students and letting them read as a group. The class can finish the selection through partner reading, or more able readers can read independently while the teacher guides the others. Then the class can move into a variety of grouping patterns (cooperative, interest, special needs, etc.) to examine the text in greater detail. Because all students have read the same selection, students of different reading achievement levels can be in the same group.

Sometimes it is not necessary for students to read the entire selection. The teacher can choose the most important segments of an expository selection and read these to or with the students. When reading a story or novel, the teacher can summarize some parts for the students and have them read only those sections that are most central to character and plot development.

Teachers should avoid reading the entire selection in one sitting, because students can easily become bored. Instead, teachers can divide the selection into short segments and process it along the way, reading the segment to or with the students and then talking about it. Teachers should use this opportunity to model good reader behaviors, thinking out loud and sharing their thoughts with the students. In this way, teachers can describe what confused them, note what they believe to be important points, and summarize the text. Teachers can connect it to their life, to other selections, or to world issues,

> **Model good reader behaviors, such as making connections with the text.**

and encourage students to do the same. It is important to avoid the question-and-answer format that is so prevalent in teacher-student discussions. Instead, teachers should talk about the selection, share their thoughts, and encourage students to do the same. Allington (2001) calls this the practice of thoughtful literacy.

It is also important to remember that a single reading of any selection is not as effective as multiple readings. Repeated reading of the same text improves word identification, fluency, and comprehension (Samuels, 1979; Carver and Hoffman, 1981; Rashotte and Torgesen, 1985; Dowhower, 1987, 1989). Therefore, classroom activities that follow the initial reading should foster repeated reading. For example, students can reread to fill out a story map or write a story summary. If the selection is expository, they can reread to fill out a semantic map or practice other forms of note taking.

Reading performance is another activity that requires repeated reading. In reading performance, students practice reading a piece of text aloud until they can read it fluently and expressively. The text can be a poem, a segment of a story, a speech, a readers' theater script, or another suitable piece. Students then perform it for their peers or for other audiences (Worthy, Broaddus, and Ivey, 2001).

How Can a Teacher Promote Strategic Reading in Whole-Group Instruction?

As we've noted, if the teacher plans ways to support reading by less able students, the teacher can use a single selection with the entire class to effectively promote strategic reading. Often we think of reading instruction as only involving three separate parts. First, the teacher prepares the students for reading by activating background or presenting crucial vocabulary. Next, the students read the selection. Finally, the students participate in some activity to assess or develop comprehension. We often forget the value of teacher modeling and student interaction *during the actual reading process.* A teacher can promote many effective strategies while the class is reading a single selection.

There are many different activities that teachers can employ when all students read the same text. For example, teachers can use the text to explore words and as a model for writing (Worthy, Broaddus, and Ivey, 2001). As well, the teacher can use a single text to present strategy lessons that are focused on questioning, inferring, visualizing, determining importance, and synthesizing (Harvey and Goudvis, 2000; Blachowicz and Ogle, 2001).

The directed reading thinking activity (DR-TA) is one strategy that has stood the test of time (Richek, 1987; Richek, Caldwell, Jennings and Lerner,

2002). The teacher stops at various points in the text and asks the students to predict what they think will happen next. The students then read on to verify their predictions and make new ones. DR-TA works for both narrative and expository text (Greenslade, 1980; Davidson, 1982).

Reciprocal teaching (Palincsar and Brown, 1984) is another effective activity for increasing strategic reading. The teacher uses a single selection and models four comprehension strategies: predicting, clarifying, finding answers to questions, and summarizing. The students gradually take over and act as teachers for the class. They model the four strategies for their classmates and encourage interaction among their peers. The teacher gently guides the process and leads all students to a greater awareness of reading strategies that can improve their comprehension.

The KWL strategy (Ogle, 1986) also lends itself to whole-class use of a single expository selection. The class first brainstorms what they know about a topic (K) and what they want to learn about it (W). The teacher and students organize the results of the brainstorming on a worksheet. The teacher then directs the students to read the selection in order to learn more about the topic (L). Instead of reading the entire selection as one unit, the teacher can stop during the reading process to note and discuss what the students learned as well as additional things they might want to learn.

Think-alouds (Leslie and Caldwell, 2001) are a reader's verbalizations in reaction to text content. Using a single text, the teacher and students read together and stop at certain prearranged points. The teacher models the process by thinking out loud and sharing reactions to the text. The teacher can paraphrase the text, make an inference, connect the text to prior knowledge or other selections, react personally, or indicate lack of understanding. The teacher then asks students to think out loud, and all share their efforts to comprehend. Think-alouds work well with both small and large groups and with oral or silent reading. The teacher needs to model the process for the students, but once they get the idea, they participate eagerly. In fact, students enjoy thinking aloud and find it far less threatening than the question-and-answer format that often follows reading. Students enjoy hearing the thoughts of others and, in the process, learn from their peers.

What Are the Characteristics of Effective Listening and Viewing in Whole-Group Instruction?

During whole-group instruction, students often listen to the teacher or to other students, or view a video or demonstration, such as a science experiment. As well, many teachers who are frustrated with student inability or unwillingness to read the text deliver the content in the form of a lecture. Unfortunately, requiring students to listen or watch without active involvement can be an ineffective form of instruction.

Teachers may improve learning through listening and viewing by utilizing techniques that focus student attention. For example, teachers can guide students to develop background knowledge, clarify important vocabulary, and raise questions that will be answered by the lecture or demonstration. Visual maps and structured overviews also focus students' attention and help them organize the information presented. As well, teachers can structure lectures or demonstrations into small sections. After each one, the teacher can form the students into small groups or pairs to tell one another what they have learned and discuss what questions they still have.

Remember that round robin oral reading is not an effective form of listening (Opitz and Rasinski, 1999). Students should not be expected to learn about the content of the text from listening to one another read parts of the text aloud. Not every child is a fluent oral reader, and this is not an effective way to develop comprehension (Masland, 1990). Students may tune out during such sessions and, as a result, comprehend very little. As well, less able readers may struggle in front of their peers. This chapter has described other more imaginative ways to structure oral reading besides a round robin format.

> **Round robin oral reading is not an effective way to develop comprehension.**

What Are the Characteristics of Effective Whole-Group Sharing of What Has Been Read or Learned?

Group sharing is based on the assumption that learning is social. Children learn from listening to and interacting with the ideas of others, and from pooling their memories, experiences, and points of view. In practice, however, whole-class discussions often fall short of this ideal (Nystrand and Gamoran, 1989).

Teachers agree that good discussions require student involvement in initiating questions and directing the course of the discussion. However, many teachers do not like to deviate from their planned topics, which can become necessary if students take over the discussion. Often, discussion is simply a teacher-dominated exercise (Mehan, 1979) characterized by a rigid questioning process that hopefully leads to a single "right" interpretation (Purvis, 1990). When class discussion reflects this transmission mode of instruction, it becomes recitation rather than true discussion (Alvermann and Dillon, 1991).

There are times when a teacher must plan a class discussion and remain in control of the process, such as when the teacher needs to set forth key ideas in order to evaluate how the students respond to them. At other times, however, an effective discussion means that the teacher follows the students' lead. Students must be responsible for initiating conversation about their reading in order to develop as independent thinkers. Because reading is an interaction between the reader and the text, and discussion provides an opportunity for offering additional perspectives, teachers must encourage student-led participation in discussion. In particular, a teacher should value the diversity, richness, and depth of multiple perspectives generated by such discussion. As well, research shows that when the teacher follows the students' lines of thought, there is greater overall reading achievement than when the teacher forges on, single-mindedly searching for a specific answer or following a teacher-designated topic (Nystrand and Gamoran, 1989).

In planning discussion questions, teachers need to go beyond the literal question with its single right answer and ask higher-level questions that are subject to multiple interpretations (Caldwell, 2002). Selections that generate thoughtful, rich, and diverse responses should be brought to the reading classroom, and teachers should encourage students to explore ideas and to set forth a variety of sound responses supported by evidence in the text. Students need to listen to one another and build on the ideas expressed by their peers. Unfortunately, students do not do this naturally. Teachers must model, probe, and scaffold responses to foster student ability to articulate a position, offer supporting evidence, and consider implications.

> **For whole-group reading instruction, choose selections that generate thoughtful, rich, and diverse responses.**

What Are the Disadvantages and Advantages of Whole-Group Instruction?

The main disadvantage of whole-class instruction is that it is often misused by ignoring the individual in favor of the group. If the teacher simplifies information, materials, and tasks or withholds concepts and activities that may be too difficult for some students, this ignores the needs of the more able students. Similarly, the needs of the less able students may be ignored if activities, materials, and tasks are too difficult.

The primary advantage of whole-class instruction is the opportunity for the entire class community to share a common text, offer their perspectives, and listen to those of their peers. Although good whole-group instruction takes much thoughtful planning on the teacher's part, if carefully executed, it can result in all learners meeting or exceeding expectations.

Under the teacher's expert facilitation, whole-group instruction can provide an opportunity for students to share personal responses to the text and consider a diversity of plausible interpretations. The teacher sets the stage by preparing the class to work together, by carefully structuring class interaction, and by selecting text that generates thoughtful, rich, and diverse responses. Of course, only classrooms that foster cooperative climates and the ethics of teamwork will be open to such instruction. Before effective whole-group instruction can take place, teachers need to build a successful classroom community.

Again whole-group reading instruction alone will never be as useful as whole-group instruction that readily switches into other flexible grouping patterns as needed. A combination of whole-group and small-group formats provides recognition of individual needs without locking the students into labels and lowered opportunities.

3

Flexible Small-Group Instruction

Different Books and Different Purposes for Different Groups

What Is Flexible Small-Group Instruction?

In classrooms of increasingly diverse students, the most critical instruction must be tailored more closely to the students' needs. One effective way to do this is to avoid an overreliance on whole-class experiences by balancing large-group instruction with the use of flexible small groups. Small groups can vary in size, age, materials, tasks, and purposes.

> Avoid an overreliance on whole-class experiences by balancing large-group instruction with the use of flexible small groups.

To accommodate all learners, the teacher uses continuous assessment to change the size and composition of the groups, the materials used with the groups, and the learning activities structured for the groups. When a group achieves the instructional goal, the teacher disbands it and creates a new group. In this way, the teacher better meets the needs of all readers. As well, students should continue to experience reading aloud, shared reading, and independent reading.

How Is This Different from the Small Groups Teachers Used in the Past?

According to the Wisconsin Department of Public Instruction (1986), "Evidence from research indicates that static grouping patterns may be less effective than flexible grouping for specific purposes" (p. 112). Remember, there is nothing inherently bad about the use of small groups during reading instruction—even the use of homogeneous small groups. It was the *inflexible use* of homogeneous small groups that caused the problems of the past. Just like the overuse of whole-group instruction can be problematic, so can the overuse of static small-group instruction.

We should also remind ourselves that the current use of small groups in reading instruction has been influenced by a philosophical and theoretical shift in our thinking. Previous use of small groups was driven by a skills-based model of reading. Groups became fixed according to perceived abilities, instruction followed a delivery model, questioning was defined by the teachers' manual, follow-up meant workbook pages, and worksheets and assessment waited until the end of units. Today, small-group reading instruction is influenced by a constructivist view of reading. Groups are flexible according to observed performances, instruction is built through scaffolded experiences, strategic questions follow the reader's lead, follow-up means practice with real reading and writing, and assessment is an ongoing, never-ending process.

The small groups in today's classroom should not look, sound, or feel like the small groups of yesterday. If they do, then we need to stand back and rethink these practices. The use of flexible small groups for reading instruction allows students to work with classmates of various skills and interests, which parallels the natural variety in groups that students will work with throughout their lives. As well, flexible grouping is a more humane procedure than rigidly classifying students according to perceived ability. In particular, changing group membership and forming groups on a basis other than ability can alleviate the many problems encountered with an emphasis on ability grouping (Anderson, Hiebert, Scott, and Wilkinson, 1985).

What Are the Purposes of Small-Group Instruction?

Teachers can form groups based on students' interests, their skill/strategy needs, and their ability to work together cooperatively and collaboratively. Certain small-group structures, including cooperative and collaborative learning, will be discussed in Chapter 5. For this chapter, we will focus on four primary purposes of small-group instruction in a reading program: to provide demonstrations, intervention, shared response for a common text and/or multiple texts, and shared inquiry. In any single reading lesson, the teacher may also plan for a combination of these purposes.

What Is the Benefit of Using Small-Group Instruction for Demonstrations?

If all demonstrations happen in large-group settings, many students—perhaps those that need them the most—may not get the specific instruction they need. As well, the teacher runs the risk of teaching both something some students do not need and something for which some students are not ready. Instead, teachers can use small groups to teach directly—demonstrate—critical procedures, literary elements, and/or skills and strategies that certain students need in a context that keeps them engaged in the instruction. For example, for students most in need of review, the teacher might use small groups to review something presented in a large group. The teacher could use another small group to introduce something for students who are ready for the new concept.

> **If all demonstrations happen in large-group settings, many students—perhaps those that need them the most—may not get the specific instruction they need.**

These small groups are usually formed by identifying students who have a similar need for the procedure, element, or strategy being demonstrated. This need has usually surfaced in the teacher's assessment of the student throughout the reading program. However, membership in the group should be temporary, especially as the students show their ability to use the instruction away from the teacher.

What Is the Benefit of Using Small Groups for Interventions?

Currently, the most popular conceptualization of small-group reading instruction is called guided reading (Fountas and Pinnell, 1996). It can be defined by five key elements. First, each group usually contains students who are more similar in their needs than they are different. An attempt is made to bring children reading at approximately the same level together for the instruction. Second, the purpose of the group is to provide students a meaning-focused, scaffolded form of instruction that acknowledges where the students are at, knows where the students need to head next, and builds a bridge between those two points. Third, the texts used for guided reading typically are at the students' instructional level. The text is within their reach but not so easy or hard it provides little opportunity for problem solving. Fourth, the teacher helps the student use strategies to move toward increasing sophistication, comfort, and confidence with the reading process. This is usually accomplished through careful ongoing assessment of students as they read, and through strategic questioning as the students talk about their reading. Finally, guided reading depends on the learner being engaged in learning as the instruction is provided.

Small groups used for intervention are usually formed by identifying students who are at similar levels in their reading development. These levels are identified through a variety of assessment techniques. Again, membership in the group should be temporary as students show growth in their development.

Guided reading is a means to an end, not an end of itself (Routman, 1999). While it is typically used with younger students, interventions may be necessary with some older students. Techniques like retrospective miscue analysis (Goodman and Marek, 1996) may provide a useful framework for providing interventions with older students. Interventions may be less critical for students who have become fairly sophisticated, independent, strategic readers.

What Is the Benefit of Using Small Groups for Shared Response?

Another popular conceptualization of small-group instruction in reading is to bring a group of readers together to share their response to a text. Sometimes the small group is focused on a single title that was read by all. At other times, the small group might be talking about a variety of titles read by members of the group. In this case, there may be a connection between these titles that focuses the discussion, or the titles may be unrelated and the discussion very open-ended. The use of small-group instruction to focus students on reading and responding to books in a social setting is at the heart of what teachers call literature circles (Daniels, 2001) or book clubs (Raphael and McMahon, 1997).

Literature circles can be composed of students who are all interested in reading and exploring the same selection or similar selections. Typically, the teacher introduces five or six books to the whole class by briefly discussing each title, author, and plot. As well, the teacher may read a brief excerpt and discuss the book's structure and difficulty. Throughout the year, the teacher challenges the students to explore new genres and subjects and to use reading to move into unexplored territory. Students choose to be part of a literature circle for personal and social reasons. Some choose a book because of individual interest or because they feel they will be able to read it successfully. Others choose a book because their friends are a part of the group and they feel comfortable sharing with them.

The membership of the literature circle may be comprised of students from mixed achievement levels. This makes it different from those groups set up for demonstrations and interventions. If students are sharing a response to a common text, the group may be more homogeneously grouped, since the chosen or assigned text may require a certain amount of reading skill. But if the shared response is structured across texts based on elements, genres, authors, topics, or themes, a more heterogeneous group may be formed. This may be one way to add flexibility to a teacher's overall grouping alternatives so that the static nature of other uses of small groups can be shaken up a bit.

Whether the teacher is present or not, small-group instruction that is focused on shared response still demands that the learner stay engaged in the learning process to receive any benefits from it. To this end, teachers assist groups in planning activities that will keep all students engaged. Groups can structure participation and discussion according to their mutual interests, or the teacher may assume a more hands-on role in monitoring and guiding the conversations to move students to more sophisticated understandings of the text. For example, teachers might encourage students to study character motivation or plot development. Group members might examine elements of a specific genre, such as fantasy or realistic fiction. They may wish to center discussion on expanding their knowledge about a different culture. They might focus discussion on how the book is like or unlike other texts they have read on the same topic. Overall, these small-group experiences provide students with the benefits from learning to listen and respond to other people's thoughts about a common reading experience.

Some would argue that this is still a form of guided reading although the teacher support is more indirect (Fawson and Reutzel, 2000). The teacher has guided the reading indirectly by assisting in the text selection, defining the response tasks, identifying the group membership, and helping the group decide how much time they will spend reading the book and how often the group will meet.

What Are the Benefits of Using Small Groups for Shared Inquiry?

Shared inquiry may be most compatible with thematic instruction. Small groups can be formed to study a theme or topic using various types of materials, including nonfiction, fiction, magazines, tapes, videos, maps, charts, diagrams,

CD-ROMs, and Internet selections. The emphasis is on learning how to learn as students increase their knowledge of the specific topic or expand their understanding of the chosen theme.

In this type of instruction, different groups may investigate specific areas related to a common topic. For example, if the topic is frogs, one group could read to learn about different types of frogs, while another might be focused on the life cycle of the frog. A third group might focus on where frogs live and what they eat. A fourth group might explore frogs in literature, such as Arnold Lobel's *Frog and Toad* series. The groups would eventually report to the class using an agreed-upon format. As well, new groups might be formed as the research continues. For example, the group investigating the life cycle of the frog might agree to split into two groups in order to learn further about the enemies of the frog throughout the life span.

Whether the groups are investigating different aspects of a common topic or different topics, the use of small groups for shared inquiry allows students to probe a subject in depth. In addition, these groups allow individuals to draw on the talents and experiences of the classmates with whom they are working to reach beyond what they might have been able to learn on their own. Students develop creativity, self-expression, perseverance, and skill in peer interaction. They assume responsibility for their own learning as they utilize research skills for discovery and independence. They also assume responsibility for group learning as they actively contribute to group goals. The teacher provides and suggests multiple resources, explains evaluation procedures for the final projects, and gently guides students to explore new areas and perhaps discover hidden talents and unknown interests.

In summary, effective use of flexible small-group instruction depends on the purpose of the experience. When the teacher is demonstrating critical skills and strategies, small groups of students with similar needs are brought together. When the teacher is providing guided reading instruction to move students forward in their reading developments, students at similar stages of development are brought together. When the teacher believes students would benefit from an opportunity to read and respond to a common book or related titles, literature groups of mixed achievement levels are formed. When the teacher wants the students to investigate important topics more independently, shared inquiry groups of students able to contribute different talents and experiences are formed.

> **The key to effective flexible grouping is to reorganize, revise, and regroup based upon careful teacher assessment of student knowledge and performance.**

Flexibility in grouping allows the teacher to enhance the self-esteem of all students and to promote interaction between diverse students. The small-group instruction methods mentioned in this chapter work well with the cooperative and collaborative structures we discuss later, as well as with more direct instruction approaches. It is vital to remember that the purpose of flexible small-group instruction is to meet the needs of the students. Therefore, groups should continually change to accommodate the interests, strengths, weaknesses, and abilities of each individual. The key to effective flexible grouping is to reorganize, revise, and regroup based upon careful teacher assessment of student knowledge and performance.

4

Individualized Reading Programs

Different Books for Each Reader

What Are the Roles of Individualized Reading Programs?

Individualized or independent reading programs should be one component of a balanced classroom literacy program, along with reading aloud, shared reading, and guided reading (Fountas and Pinnell, 1996). Individualized reading programs have also been conceptualized as a critical part of a language arts block that includes guided reading, writing workshop, and working with words (Cunningham, Hall, and Defee, 1991). Individualized reading programs tend to serve one of two primary purposes: recreation or instruction. An example of an individualized program that is focused on reading as recreation is sustained silent reading (SSR), a classroom time when students read books of their choice without interruption for instruction or discussion. Sustained silent reading programs include Drop Everything and Read (DEAR) and Super Quiet Uninterrupted Reading Time (SQUIRT). In these programs, the focus is providing students access, choice, and opportunities to experience reading as a recreational activity. There is less focus on seizing the experiences for instructional purposes. While such programs have the potential to impact on students' skills, strategies, and dispositions, typically only minimal accountability is built in. Promoting the joy of the reading habit is the primary outcome (Pilgreen, 2000).

> **Individualized programs with more of an instructional focus allow teachers to tailor reading instruction to individual students.**

In contrast, individualized programs with more of an instructional focus allow teachers to tailor reading instruction to individual students. They offer a viable alternative to traditional ability-grouped reading programs and allow teachers to overcome the difficulties inherent in whole-group instruction (Berghoff and Egawa, 1991). In the past, individualized reading programs were designed under the influence of skills-based models of reading. However, current models of individualized reading programs that are focused on instructional purposes have embraced a more process-oriented style of reading instruction. This type of program honors the access, choice, and opportunity of recreational programs while recognizing the potential instructional opportunities from these experiences.

What Is Process-Oriented Reading Instruction?

Process-oriented reading programs are modeled after process-oriented writing programs (Atwell, 1998; Hansen, 2001). They are often called reading workshop programs. In process-oriented programs, sustained reading is placed within an instructional framework.

Three primary elements in process-oriented literacy programs are time, choice, and response. Students are provided with significant blocks of time to read books. Because these approaches are based on a learn-by-doing philosophy, students spend their time reading instead of studying about reading. Students are also allowed to choose what they read and how they respond to it. This often means that each student is reading a different book and may respond in different ways. As well, response includes sharing with others by meeting with the teacher and peers to conference about what students are reading. In this way, response often distinguishes process-oriented instructional programs from sustained silent reading recreational programs.

How Is Time Structured in a
Reading Workshop Program?

While formats for reading workshop programs vary, they are often structured around five key elements: focus lessons, sustained reading, response, conferencing, and sharing. A typical reading block would be divided so that adequate time is allowed for each of those elements, with much of the time devoted to sustained reading and conferencing.

What Are Focus Lessons?

Focus lessons, also called minilessons, are short, whole-group, teacher-directed lessons. They are often conducted at the beginning of the reading workshop. Focus lessons usually last about five to ten minutes and are developed according to the needs of the students. There are three types of focus lessons: procedural, literary, and skill/strategy.

Procedural focus lessons involve discussions about the actual procedures used in the reading workshop. The class might discuss how to fill out the reading log form or how to cooperate better during peer sharing time.

Literary focus lessons expose children to different titles, authors, genres, story elements, and stylistic techniques. These focus lessons encourage students to choose different books or books of better quality. They help readers focus on certain literary aspects of the books they are reading.

The teacher designs the skill/strategy focus lessons around the needs of the readers. These lessons may introduce readers to using a balanced set of strategies to figure out words, or to using comprehension strategies to process a variety of texts.

> **Focus lessons, or minilessons, are short, whole-group, teacher-directed lessons. They are often conducted at the beginning of the reading workshop.**

How Much Time Should Be Set Aside for Sustained Reading?

Sustained reading time often depends on the age, ability, and experience of the readers. Older students will stay engaged for longer periods of time than younger and less experienced readers. Teachers may want to start with a relatively small block of time and gradually increase it as students seem more able to stay engaged.

What Is the Best Way to Keep All Readers Engaged During This Time?

Teachers should begin by modeling the reading process. The teacher's engagement might be a good example for students. If many students are having difficulty staying engaged, teachers can reduce the time allotment for the sustained reading and then gradually build it up. If just a few students have trouble staying engaged, they can be moved closer to the teacher. Sometimes the teacher may need to quietly read to or with a student during this time. Younger readers should be allowed to have more than one book near them during this time.

Simple accountability procedures help students know they will be responsible for what they did during this time. Some teachers use a "status of the class" activity to quickly find out what students are doing. The teacher keeps a class list nearby and records what the students say they are reading. If engagement is a problem, teachers can raise the issue as a procedural focus lesson and let the students help in discovering other solutions. Remember, the only way a learn-to-read-by-reading approach works is if the students are engaged in reading. If this time is set aside and the students do not read, it will be difficult for them to get better at reading.

What If Students Do Not Make Appropriate Choices in Selecting Their Books for Reading Workshop?

Four issues often surface when teachers think about choice in independent reading programs: difficulty, variety, quality, and access. While some teachers may feel more comfortable narrowing the choices so that students will choose an appropriate text, a better instructional strategy is to teach students how to make good choices. Teachers can provide students with a simple framework to judge a book's difficulty level for themselves (Ohlhausen and Jepsen, 1992):

Challenge books are books that are too hard for the student, even with help from others. Students shouldn't be discouraged from seeking out these books because they can become incentives for improving at reading, but they should also choose a more appropriate leveled book for reading time.

Easy books are books that the student can read without any difficulty. They are valuable for developing fluency and confidence.

"*Books I'm Working On*" may be best suited for use during reading workshop. These are just right for reading with the teacher during a conference and provide the possibility of strategic instruction (Hansen, 2001).

What Is the Best Way to Encourage Variety in the Habits of Some Students Who Choose to Read the Same Types of Books Over and Over?

First, teachers should utilize focus lesson time to expose students to a wide variety of works. This sets out invitations for students to venture into new areas with their reading. Second, students should be allowed to share with one another. Peer enthusiasm for a book may cause a student to pick up a new title. Third, during meetings with individual students, teachers should discuss this issue as goals are set. Finally, some teachers do build in expectations that students read a variety of texts by using simple tools to help students keep track of the types of books they are reading. These tools also remind students of the many types of texts that are available for reading. For example, teachers can create a handout with a wheel on it, labeling the sections on the wheel with different genres. When students have read from a genre, they color in that part of the wheel.

How Can Teachers Encourage Students to Read Works of Greater Quality?

Teachers can use literary focus lessons to expose students to quality works as well as to ways to analyze the quality of the works they are reading. For example, one focus lesson could highlight the language authors use to convey a sense of the setting. Teachers can invite students to examine their texts for good examples of setting language. Students with plot-driven novels may have difficulty finding rich, descriptive language. When they share, these students will discover that the language chosen by their authors usually pales in comparison to the language of more celebrated authors such as Gary Paulsen, Patricia MacLachlan, or Sterling North. In this way, students will begin to realize that the quality of writing does differ in books. As well, selections used for read-alouds, whole-group instruction, and/or literature circles may be other ways to guarantee that all readers get exposed to a variety of quality texts.

How Can Teachers Acquire Enough Books to Meet Student Needs?

Some researchers have estimated that reading workshop programs need to build on a minimum of ten titles per child in the classroom. Teachers have discovered a wide variety of ways to build up their classroom libraries. If possible, teachers can order trade books with funds that are not being used to purchase other commercial reading materials. If allowed, book clubs provide easy access to relatively inexpensive titles. Used bookstores and garage sales can also supplement the supply.

Teachers can also include class-made materials in the library corner. The class can solicit donations of used books or books on loan from the students' families. In other words, teachers should tap any available source to get books, being sure to consider books for various ability levels and interests.

What Happens During the Response Period of Reading Workshop?

Time is set aside for all readers to respond to their texts. Often, response occurs through the use of writing in journals. Students are asked to log in what they read for the day and respond to it. Some teachers are more comfortable using a structured format that causes all readers to respond in similar ways each day. Other teachers give readers a choice in the way they respond, including options besides writing. Structures may vary, but response is key for building accountability into the process. It provides the opportunity for instruction and creates a paper trail for assessment. The format for the response may be less critical than providing time for response.

Structures may vary, but response is key for building accountability into the process.

How Does Conferencing Work in the Reading Workshop Program?

There are two important conferencing formats: peer conferences and teacher conferences. Peers meet together to share what they have been reading and how they have been responding. Usually, teacher conferences are a time for the students to meet individually with the teacher. These conferences are critical to maintain ongoing assessment and instruction.

In order for the teacher to find the time to conference with individuals, the other students must stay engaged. Therefore, an effective peer conference structure engages most students so that the teacher can sit down individually with other students. As well, some teachers have set up a number of response project options on which students can work independently. For example, students can always continue their independent reading and writing as a way of staying engaged while the teacher works with another student.

What Are Some Ways to Establish Effective Formats for Peer Conferences?

Some teachers develop routines that are easy for students to carry out on their own. One teacher invited her fifth graders to meet in their cooperative learning teams. They quietly passed their response journals to the other members of their team. Each team member read what had been written and responded to it in writing. After each team member responded to each journal, the journals were returned to their original owners, who read what had been written. After everyone read the responses, the group moved into an oral discussion about what they had read and written.

Such routines can vary, and not all routines may be suitable for all age levels. Younger readers may only be capable of sharing with a partner. At that level, the peer conference may not be a critical part of the reading workshop program.

Teachers may want to use focus lesson time to introduce conferencing procedures, create guidelines, and discuss improvements for peer conferencing. For example, during a focus lesson, the teacher can model effective conferences. Similarly, role-playing may allow students to see good examples of peer conferences. The teacher may ask a group of students to try a peer conference "in a fishbowl" so that others can watch and analyze what they see.

What Happens During the Teacher Conference?

The teacher has two primary tasks: to assess and to instruct based on that assessment. The nature of the conference will vary with the reader's age and ability level. With beginning readers, teachers may want to drop in on the oral reading of the child, utilizing an assessment technique such as a running record (Clay, 1993). With advanced readers, the focus shifts to discussing the book and the response, and determining whether instruction would assist the reader in more effectively interpreting texts. The conference also provides a time for teachers to assist the students in setting goals and evaluating progress toward goals. Finally, it provides an opportunity for the student and teacher to have enthusiastic conversations about books.

The reading conference results in valuable information to inform the teacher's instructional and assessment decisions. Many teachers develop a system to record information obtained during the conference. Some have a folder for each child. When the teacher confer-ences with the child, this folder is nearby and used as a place to record or file information. Others keep a three-ring binder containing a section for each child. Recording information over time in systems like these allows teachers to see patterns in the individual performances of students and make better instructional and assessment decisions. This helps teachers see what might be the focus of the next conference. These systems also allow teachers to see patterns across students, which provides a basis for decisions about focus lessons.

> **The reading conference results in valuable information to inform the teacher's instructional and assessment decisions.**

How Often Should Teachers Meet with Students?

The best answer is as often as possible. However, even if a quality conference lasted only five to ten minutes, a teacher would be able to complete only a few conferences a day. Obviously, a teacher needs to schedule conferences so all students have interaction with the teacher during a given time period. Students of concern may need to rotate through the schedule more often than others.

In addition to conferences, teachers can use other techniques to make regular contact with students. They may collect response journals or student portfolios for review, and provide individualized instruction through written response to this material. Teachers can also meet with a small group of students with similar needs, thereby increasing the number of students seen during the conference time.

Teachers may need to catch some students during transitional times, such as when they are coming into the classroom in the morning or after recess. Teachers may also decide to do more informal conferences by moving from desk to desk where the children are working instead of asking students to come to a conferencing center.

How Do Teachers Hold a Conference with Students If the Teachers Haven't Read the Books?

Years ago, teachers were led to believe that they should read every book placed in an individualized reading program. They were told to instructionally prepare each book for the reader. Those preparations often became the basis for the conference with the student. However, because of the commitment to choice in reading workshop programs, this would be an impossible task.

In reading workshop, teachers do not prepare every book for instruction. This change is partially due to our shift from a focus on skills, such as knowing individual words and ascertaining the content of individual texts, to a focus on strategies, such as how to figure out unknown words and how to better understand texts. During conferences, generic strategies about processing text can form a frame for discussing almost any text. Instead of checking to see if the student knows the meaning of a specific word from the story, the teacher can ask the student to tell about a confusing word in the story and discuss which strategies could be used to figure it out.

Likewise, questions to assess comprehension of a specific text are less important than general questions about how a student processes text. During a conference, without knowing the exact content of the book, a teacher can get a sense of whether the student uses common narrative elements such as setting, characterization, or conflict to help reach a deeper understanding of the text. When reading is seen as more of a transaction between the reader and the text, it becomes more of a personal act in which the reader's interpretation—not just securing one right meaning—becomes the focus of the discussion about the text. It is to the advantage of teachers using reading workshop to have an extensive knowledge of children's books, but it is also refreshing when the teacher is allowed to be a naive learner—to know nothing about the text—so the student can teach the teacher. This allows the teacher's questions to be genuine inquiry from an interested learner, not an inquisition to hold students accountable for what they have read.

What Happens During the Sharing Time of Reading Workshop?

Reading workshop advocates the social construction of knowledge and the building of a community of readers. Sharing allows these goals to develop. Sharing can be done informally with partners or in small groups, but there is also value in encouraging students to share formally with the entire community. Teachers should also seize this opportunity to share who they are as readers and show that they value reading in their lives.

Is It Necessary to Use Reading Workshop as the Entire Reading Program?

While reading workshop forms the heart of some teachers' entire reading programs, independent reading is just one component of a balanced literacy program. Teachers who have not tried reading workshop may want to start small. They can pick one day a week for doing reading workshop and integrate it with existing reading instruction. Or they can set aside a little time each day to do reading workshop. Starting small may allow teachers to get comfortable with a process-oriented reading program to see how quickly they could move in that direction.

> **Versions of reading workshop have been used successfully at all grade levels.**

Is Reading Workshop Appropriate for All Grades?

The classrooms described later in this book reveal that versions of reading workshop have been used successfully at all grade levels. One size does not fit all, however, and teachers have developed different versions of this model to best suit the readers with whom they are working (MacKenzie, 1992; Marriott, 2002; Serafini, 2001).

What If Teachers Are More Comfortable with a More Structured Reading Program? Are There Any Ways to Adapt This Model?

Focused workshops (Jett-Simpson, 1991) allow readers the flexibility of still being able to choose from a variety of texts, but they assist the teacher in narrowing down the instructional focus for the reading period. Teachers can provide a focus so what students are reading and how they are responding are similar. This may include selecting a specific genre, such as mysteries, or the same topic, such as the frontier. Again, students still have some choice in selecting books, but the teacher has a common basis for making decisions about focus lessons, response activities, and conferencing.

In its purest form, reading workshop takes on a studio atmosphere. Time is set aside and students independently engage in the process of reading and responding. Students may be at different points in the process and engaged in doing different things at the same time. However, teachers more comfortable with an externally structured reading program can adapt the model so it works more effectively for the community of readers in their classroom.

5

Cooperative Grouping

Mixed Groups for a Common Purpose

What Is Cooperative Grouping?

The expression "two heads are better than one" is familiar to all of us. We can all think of examples of how working together resulted in a better product than if we had worked in isolation. Whether the example is developing curriculum or planning lessons, we know that discussing ideas and working with colleagues can help stimulate thinking.

Cooperative grouping involves having students work together in small heterogeneous groups to accomplish a common goal or team task (Harp, 1989; Opitz, 1992). The teacher carefully structures the group task so that all students are clear about the goal and the group procedures. Because the task is clear to everyone in the group, each member is able to contribute to the common goal. The typical composition of a cooperative team is four or five boys and girls with a balance of high, average, and low achieving students.

What Are Typical Characteristics of Most Cooperative Learning Models?

Most cooperative learning involves five basic characteristics (Johnson, Johnson, Holubec, and Roy, 1984):

- Positive interdependence
- Face-to-face interaction
- Individual accountability

- Interpersonal and small-group skills
- Group processing

Positive interdependence means that students recognize they truly need each other to complete the group task or project. The teacher fosters such interdependence through setting mutual goals, offering joint rewards, and assigning roles to group members (the recorder, the summarizer, the encourager, etc.). Face-to-face interaction occurs as students promote each other's learning by sharing, encouraging, explaining, and discussing. Individual accountability happens as the teacher assesses the performance of each group member, and their individual scores contribute to the group score.

As well, cooperative learning will not work if students do not have interpersonal and small-group skills. Recognizing this, teachers teach such skills as precisely and purposefully as they teach a comprehension strategy. They model and foster leadership, decision making, trust building, communication, and conflict management skills. Finally, group processing means giving groups both time and procedures for analyzing how well the group is functioning. Is the group achieving their goal? Is the group maintaining an effective working relationship among members?

How Is Cooperative Grouping Used in Instruction?

There are four parts to a cooperative lesson (Harp, 1989):

- Teacher instruction
- Teacher formation of groups and setting of objectives
- Students working together
- Evaluation

The first part is teacher instruction. The teacher begins by teaching new content or modeling a strategy or process. This is often directed to the class as a whole. Next, the teacher forms cooperative groups and sets academic and cooperative objectives. The teacher gives specific directions as to procedures and explains evaluation processes. Third, students work together to complete a task assigned to the group. They work on individual assignments that contribute to the overall group assignment. As the group members interact, the teacher carefully monitors progress and intervenes as necessary to provide task assistance or to teach and reinforce cooperative skills.

The fourth part of the cooperative lesson is evaluation. The teacher evaluates both the individual group members and the group as a whole. Each group member is accountable for his or her achievement. In addition, an individual's score or grade is combined with that of other team members to produce a group grade. The groups themselves are part of the evaluation as group members discuss how well the group functioned and what improvements could be made. Groups that meet their goals receive some form of prearranged recognition for their performance.

What Are Some Advantages of Cooperative Grouping?

Research suggests that there are many advantages of cooperative grouping:

- Increased student achievement
- Development of interpersonal skills
- Development of independence
- Increased positive attitude toward schooling
- Increased self-esteem and social skills

Children in cooperative groups tend to demonstrate greater achievement than children in other grouping formats (Jongsma, 1990; Opitz, 1992; Slavin, 1982, 1988; Johnson and Johnson, 1984). Students working in cooperative groups produce more and better ideas than individuals working alone. As well, students develop interpersonal and small-group interaction skills. They are more likely to help each other in cooperative formats, and they seem to become more tolerant of others' differences. Furthermore, students in cooperative groups become less dependent on the teacher and express more positive attitudes toward learning, the teachers, and their own work. They tend to reinforce positive school norms, such as reminding each other to complete their work. Finally, cooperative grouping has a positive effect on students' self-esteem and social skills (Slavin, 1991).

> **Children in cooperative groups tend to demonstrate greater achievement than children in other grouping formats.**

What Are Some of the Problems Associated with Cooperative Grouping?

One frequently expressed concern about group work deals with student participation. Will everyone participate or will one or two students do all the work? A learning group is not truly cooperative if a few individuals dominate. To ensure that all members learn and participate, the teacher needs to observe progress toward the common goal, note individual participation, and provide goal clarification to students who need assistance.

Developing successful self-managed teams in which all members contribute to the common goal is a difficult task. Again, one common problem is lack of participation on the part of one or two students. An equally difficult problem is the situation in which one or two members try to dominate all decision making and product development. Students need assistance in learning how to participate effectively in cooperative groups. Students need time and careful guidance to acquire techniques that can help them reach their common group goal.

Teachers also need to learn how to set up cooperative learning and design activities that facilitate group learning. Cooperative learning is not something that can be quickly implemented. It takes much time and planning.

Are Cooperative Groups Different from Collaborative Groups?

The difference between cooperative and collaborative grouping depends on the purpose of the group. If students in a group are responsible for producing individual products and are evaluated individually, then this type of group work is collaborative. In collaborative grouping, students may influence their peers, but they do not control the individual efforts. If, however, students are responsible for the product as a group and a team score is part of the evaluation, then the group can be called cooperative.

It is an error to label tutoring sessions as cooperative learning. In cooperative learning, all group members are equally important in making decisions, learning material, and producing a product. In a tutoring session, one member dominates as the tutor. Peer tutoring can be effective but it is not cooperative learning as defined in the research literature.

What Are Some Specific Cooperative Activities That Teachers Might Try in the Classroom?

There are three approaches to cooperative learning that have been researched: Student Teams Achievement Division (Slavin and Karweit, 1981; Madden and Slavin, 1983; Slavin, 1982, 1983); Teams Games Tournament (Stallings and Stipek, 1985; Slavin, 1983; Slavin and Karweit, 1981; DeVries and Slavin, 1978); and Jigsaw II (Slavin, 1983). These three techniques eliminate problems associated with cooperative grouping by making the group's success contingent upon each member's success.

In Student Teams Achievement Division (STAD), the teacher presents a new lesson to the class. Students then work together to study the content or learn the new skill. For example, the teacher might present a lesson on new vocabulary, and the group members would work through a vocabulary activity. If the lesson focused on certain prefixes, suffixes, or roots, then the students would review their meanings. The teacher directs the students to study until all group members understand the information. The teacher then assesses the students individually with similar activities. The team score is determined by calculating the extent to which each student has improved over past efforts. Students who exceed their own past performance and teams with high overall scores receive recognition. STAD allows lower-achieving students to contribute the most points to their team by showing improvement.

In Teams Games Tournament (TGT), students also study together, but instead of taking individual quizzes, they play academic games with students of similar ability. For example, the high performers in Team A compete with the high performers in Team B and Team C. The same type of tournament competition occurs for average and low performers. Individuals contribute their scores to the total team score. The games often involve answering questions pertaining to the material being studied, and groups conduct regular practice sessions with teammates to help each other locate and remember the answers to key questions. For example, if the topic is the American Revolution, groups use the text to formulate possible questions and answers for the academic tournament that will follow. After the practice sessions, students move to different tournament tables and compete with representatives from other groups. Players compare scores and, as in STAD, top scorers are recognized.

Jigsaw II is an adaptation of a cooperative technique developed by Aronson (1978). Aronson's technique, Jigsaw I, involves cooperative groups of five or six members. Each group member accepts responsibility for teaching one part of a lesson to the other group members. To determine the most effective way to present their lesson part, all students working on the same part join a different group. This group discusses and prepares effective strategies for teaching their segment. For example, if the topic of the lesson is the solar system, the teacher assigns one planet to each group member. All students who are responsible for presenting information on Mars to their groups form a new cooperative group. They research Mars and discuss effective ways of presenting this information to their peers. After they complete their preparation, they return to their original group, and each member presents his or her part of the lesson. In order to understand the entire lesson, group members must listen to the information their teammates have prepared.

In Jigsaw II (Slavin, 1983), all team members read the same text, such as a book chapter, a short story, or a biography. Then, each student receives a topic on which to become the expert. For example, the teacher decides to use a Jigsaw format for story analysis or discussion. Each student receives one of the following topics to research and present to the group: how setting influenced the plot; how the main character changed from the beginning of the story until the end; how minor characters influenced the main character; what the primary problem was and how it was resolved; and how this story compares to previously read selections. Students assigned the same topic meet together and prepare their presentation. Then they return to their teams to teach the information they have learned and prepared. The teacher quizzes all teams, determines individual and team scores, and recognizes high performers.

Uttero (1988) describes another cooperative model that is directly focused on reading instruction. The three phases of the model are connection, guided independent reading, and follow-up. The connection phase includes activities designed to activate prior knowledge and to help students relate new information to the knowledge they already possess. Some of these activities involve cooperative groups of students brainstorming ideas related to key vocabulary, categorizing ideas through semantic mapping, comparing and contrasting objects and ideas, and listing what they already know about a topic. In the guided independent reading phase, students work together to interpret the text. They read together in pairs or larger cooperative groups, and they are encouraged to react and respond while reading. Activities might involve thinking aloud with groups of students, paraphrasing sections of the text in order to demonstrate their understanding, asking questions, constructing possible answers, making inferences, and reacting personally. In the follow-up stage, students summarize the text and apply their knowledge to new contexts. Groups present and revise their summaries and reactions to other groups.

Another cooperative learning technique recommended for middle and high school students is group retellings (Wood, 1987). Students work in groups of three or more, with each individual reading different information about a common topic. Students read their material and prepare to retell it to their team members. For example, if students were studying information related to community improvement, some individuals could read newspaper editorials or locate relevant material on the Web. Other students could read textbook selections or magazine articles. The students would then come together to share with their teammates what they had learned.

Can Cooperative or Collaborative Learning Be Applied to Other Forms of Grouping?

The basic concept of cooperative and collaborative grouping lends itself to integration within other grouping alternatives. In Chapter 3, we described oral and silent partner reading, also called dyad reading. In that activity, the elements of cooperation and collaboration are clearly evident as students work together to figure out unknown words, recall and summarize the text, and clarify what was read. After students read or listen to the same text or participate in whole-group instruction, the teacher can foster collaboration by such devices as Think-Pair-Share (Lyman, 1988) and Turn-to-Your-Neighbor (Reutzel, 1999). In Think-Pair-Share, children individually think of an answer and then discuss this with their partner. The final answer reflects consensus between them or a new answer constructed from their collaborative efforts. In Turn-to-Your-Neighbor, students simply turn to their neighbor and share their reactions to what was read or presented.

> The basic concept of cooperative and collaborative grouping lends itself to integration within other grouping alternatives.

In Chapter 3, we discussed small-group instruction in which students read the same text and come together to retell, summarize, and share perspectives. Reutzel (1999) suggests that this is effective with a group of three students, which is called a focus trio. Group retellings also work when students read different selections and present what they learned to their peers. Group members then offer comments, request clarification, or relate the selection to the text they read. The elements of positive interdependence, face-to-face interaction, and interpersonal skills are evident in many grouping formats.

What Are Some Tips to Ensure Successful Cooperative Group Learning?

It is important to form cooperative groups that reflect the makeup of the classroom. Groups should contain a balance of high-, middle-, and low-ability students; different ethnic groups; and boys and girls. The teacher should vary group size based upon the purposes for the group and create, change, or disband groups on a systematic basis to meet specific goals.

> **Cooperative groups should reflect the makeup of the classroom.**

The teacher must help students develop group interaction skills and provide time for them to practice group techniques. It takes a lot of time and effort for all students to become effective members of a group. The teacher should observe group interaction on a regular basis and highlight positive, successful interactions among students. The teacher can also foster self-evaluation among groups by regularly asking them to assess their own interaction skills. Students must attain some skill in working together before their academic learning will be positively affected.

The teacher should structure group tasks and activities that are appropriate to the needs and interests of the team members. As well, team members need opportunities to participate in identifying group goals. The teacher should discuss how the group work is related to the overall curriculum and provide clear directions that are readily available so students can refer to them if they forget. It is also important to provide many opportunities for students to evaluate and recognize their progress and how it relates to the accomplishment of the group's goals.

In summary, two heads are often better than one, but this is only true to the extent that cooperative activities are carefully planned and sensitively nurtured. Cooperative learning is not a quick fix. It takes a lot of time on the teacher's part and a lot of effort on the students' part, but it can be an exciting and effective grouping format and a worthy alternative to ability grouping.

6

Paired Grouping

Partners for Many Purposes

What Is Paired Grouping?

Paired grouping, often called partner grouping, occurs when two students work together to read a selection or to accomplish a task. The pairs are usually of mixed achievement levels. Paired grouping is an effective supplement to other classroom grouping arrangements and provides additional occasions for students of all reading levels to improve comprehension, fluency, and learning. The teacher can easily incorporate paired grouping into the regular classroom reading program once sufficient modeling and guidance have been provided to students.

. . . .

Paired grouping can supplement other classroom grouping arrangements and provides additional occasions for students of all reading levels to improve.

. . . .

What Are the Different Formats of Paired Grouping?

There are a variety of paired grouping formats, depending on the purpose for the pairing. One of the most common is paired reading used as a vehicle for peer tutoring. This originated as a technique for parents so they could assist their children at home (Topping, 1987). However, the format of the original technique has been successfully taught to peer tutors as a method of supporting their partners through texts that would otherwise be too difficult. Sometimes these tutors come from cross-age arrangements made between classrooms at different grade levels. The teacher can also use paired grouping for repeated reading practice and to improve reading and learning in the content areas.

What Are Some Guidelines for Using Paired Grouping in Peer Tutoring?

Usually, a more able reader is paired with a less able one for the purpose of tutoring. In this arrangement, the reading skills of tutors improve as much or more than that of the tutees (Sharpley and Sharpley, 1981). Additionally, both members of the tutoring pair tend to improve in social relationships and attitudes toward reading (Topping, 1989).

Although there are several variations of peer tutoring, they share certain critical elements (Limbrick, McNaughton, and Cameron, 1985; Topping, 1988):

1. The competence of the tutor in relationship to the tutee is a critical consideration. The teacher should control differences in ability so that the tutor is not understimulated. However, the tutor must be skilled enough to provide the necessary support to the tutee.

2. The teacher should consider student preferences and social relationships when selecting pairs. Same-sex partners tend to be preferred, but "mixed-sex matching is not consistently associated with lesser learning gains" (Topping, 1989, p. 490).

3. Reading materials should be interesting to both the tutor and the tutee, but must not be too difficult for the tutor. In the beginning, teacher guidance will probably be necessary to help pairs select appropriate materials.

4. Peer tutoring requires training. The teacher should train each pair separately and should model the desired behaviors. Only a few pairs should be trained at a time so the teacher can provide adequate supervision.

5. Tutoring sessions should last for a minimum of fifteen minutes but should not exceed thirty minutes.

6. Tutoring sessions should occur at least three times per week.

7. The tutoring relationship should last for approximately six weeks. In this way, both partners become fluent and practiced in the procedure and can transfer their skill to another partner. However, the teacher

should terminate the relationship while both members still find it interesting and rewarding.

8. Pairs should be monitored and evaluated. The teacher needs to keep a close eye on how things are going. For evaluation purposes, the teacher should use some type of pre- and post-assessment. Running records or an informal reading inventory are useful tools for this purpose.

9. Parental agreement is important. The teacher should inform parents of both tutor and tutee of the potential benefits for the students.

How Do Teachers Implement Paired Grouping for Peer Tutoring?

Limbrick, McNaughton, and Cameron (1985) outlined specific steps for peer tutors to apply during paired reading:

1. The tutee selects a book with the help of the tutor. The teacher should set aside a box of suitable books for this purpose.

2. The tutor and tutee settle themselves in a quiet, predetermined place.

3. The tutor and tutee discuss the book by looking at the title, the cover, and the author's name. If they are continuing a story from the previous day, they review what has happened and make predictions about future events.

4. The tutor and tutee begin reading aloud together. They agree on a starting signal such as "1, 2, 3 . . . " The tutor adjusts to the tutee's natural reading speed. If the tutee desires to read independently, he or she signals this to the tutor. For example, the tutee might knock on the table twice and, when this happens, the tutor stops reading and allows the tutee to continue. If the tutee makes an error, the tutor begins to read along again until the tutee once again signals to read independently.

5. If the tutee hesitates on a word, the tutor does not intervene for five seconds. The tutor then says the word, and the tutee repeats it and continues to read. Tutors often tend to correct the tutees too quickly, even though they have been instructed to wait five seconds before doing so. The teacher should teach the tutor to raise the fingers on one hand one at a time while simultaneously whispering the numbers one through five to themselves. When all fingers on the hand are raised, they can repeat the word correctly to the tutee. This wait time gives the

tutee a better opportunity to come up with the word independently before receiving assistance.

6. The tutor waits until the end of a sentence before providing help if the tutee makes an error. The tutor does not consider self-corrections and repetitions as errors.

7. The tutor gives praise for correct reading at regular intervals.

8. At the end of approximately ten to fifteen minutes of reading, the tutor and tutee briefly discuss the book together. The teacher can use a kitchen timer to keep the pairs on task and within the predetermined time limit. After they situate themselves in their designated location and are ready to begin, they set the timer for twenty minutes. When the timer rings, the pairs know to stop immediately and put their materials away. The timer should not face the tutor and tutee; this discourages "clock watching."

9. The tutee returns the book to the box and the tutor fills in a report card that provides a record of how the session went.

Peer tutoring using paired grouping can be a highly successful program for all readers if certain components are carefully considered. These components are discussed next.

Number of Pairs

A tutoring session can be most manageable when a maximum of three pairs meet during each six-week period. This allows the teacher to monitor the pairs closely and evaluate the progress being made by both tutor and tutee. This also builds eagerness for the other students to participate when it becomes their turn. It is important that all students eventually participate in paired reading. During peer tutoring, the remainder of the class either reads individually or with a reading buddy using self-selected reading materials at their independent reading levels.

> **Peer tutoring using shared grouping can be a highly successful program for all readers.**

Selection of Pairs

Selection of pairs requires great care. The teacher should not implement peer tutoring immediately during the first weeks of school. Instead, the teacher needs time to get to know the class and to assess each student's reading ability, interests, and social skills. At the end of this initial get-acquainted period, the teacher should rank order the students according to their overall reading ability. From this ranking, the teacher can pick the first three pairs for training.

It is not effective to pair the top student with the bottom student. Too much difference in reading ability causes the top student to be bored and the bottom student to be uncomfortable. Rather, the teacher should divide the rank-ordered class into two groups and pair the top reader in the first group with the top reader in the second group. For example, in a class of twenty-four students, the reader ranked number one would be paired with the reader ranked number thirteen. Of course, this ordering does not necessarily guarantee a good match. The teacher should also consider the sex of the partners and other social aspects. Boys tend to prefer being with boys and vice versa. The pairings will be more successful if the students share common interests and enjoy each other's company.

Parental Understanding

Parental understanding and permission is important to the success of the program. The teacher must explain the concept of peer tutoring to parents and assure them of reading growth for both tutor and tutee. The teacher should encourage parents to call with any questions or concerns they might have.

What Are Some Other Forms of Paired Grouping?

Paired Repeated Reading

One form of paired grouping is paired repeated reading, an adaptation of repeated reading (Samuels, 1979). It is a repetition strategy that improves oral fluency and comprehension when used as part of regular reading instruction (Koskinen and Blum, 1984, 1986).

Each student counts out approximately fifty words from a passage at the reader's independent reading level. For the sake of interest and to discourage comparison, each student selects a different passage. The first reader reads his or her passage out loud three consecutive times. At the end of each reading, the reader fills out a self-evaluation sheet. While the reader is reading, the listener listens actively. The teacher may have to demonstrate how to be an attentive listener. The listener praises noted reading improvement and may fill out listening sheets for the second and third readings. Then the students switch roles.

A typical paired repeated reading session takes place with a partner for ten to fifteen minutes. As with peer tutoring, teacher guidance for working in pairs is critical.

Reading Buddies

Reading buddies is another form of paired reading. A more able reader can be a buddy to a less able reader and provide support through a difficult piece of text. Cunningham, Hall and Defee (1991) recommend this strategy for the guided reading segment of her four-block instructional plan for teaching reading without using ability groups. Similarly, readers of like ability can be paired as reading buddies to read and discuss material. It is possible for an entire class to read with their buddies at the same time as long as students read and discuss in a quiet voice with predetermined seating arrangements. Initially, the teacher may have to model appropriate buddy behavior. Reading buddy time also provides a perfect opportunity for the teacher to move from pair to pair and collect observational data on reading growth.

How Can Paired Grouping Help Students to Improve Reading and Learning in the Content Areas?

The teacher can effectively use heterogeneous pairs to facilitate reading and learning in the content areas. Manarino-Leggett and Salomon (1989) suggest the following paired grouping formats.

Dyads. Students work in pairs to read and study content area material (Wood, 1987; Madden, 1988). The pairs begin by silently reading approximately two pages of text. One partner is assigned the role of recaller and the other has the role of listener. The recaller summarizes orally what has been read. It is the job of the listener to correct, clarify, and elaborate on what has been stated. Partners then switch roles for the next two pages. An entire chapter may be read using this process.

Summary Pairs. Pairs alternate orally reading and summarizing paragraphs of text. One partner reads and summarizes. The other partner listens, checks the text for accuracy, and adds anything left out. Partners alternate roles after each paragraph.

Think-Pair-Share. Assigned pairs sit together during a lesson presentation. At the end of the lesson, the teacher asks a question or series of questions. Each student first thinks of an answer and then shares this with his or her partner. The partners work to reach consensus on an answer and then share the agreed-upon answer with the class (Lyman, 1988).

Paired Retellings. Students work in pairs, with each partner reading a different text on the same topic. After reading, partners retell in their own words (Cunningham, 1988). A follow-up activity is to join one pair with another pair and repeat the retellings.

Focus Pairs. Before reading, pairs summarize what they already know about a topic and come up with questions they may have. After reading, the pairs discuss the new information, answer their questions, and formulate new ones.

Skill Pairs. Pairs work together on specific skills that need practice until both partners can perform it consistently or explain it easily.

Composition Pairs. Pairs help each other during the pre-writing assignment. The first partner explains what he or she plans to write while the second partner takes notes on this or makes an outline. They plan an opening statement together. Then the roles are reversed. Partners exchange outlines and use them to write their papers.

Book Report Pairs. Student pairs interview each other about a book they have read. They then report on their partner's book to the rest of the class.

What Are the Disadvantages and Advantages of Paired Grouping?

The disadvantages of paired grouping, like any form of grouping, involve the careful planning that is needed by the teacher to ensure successful implementation. Children do not always know how to work together effectively. The teacher must model, foster, and reinforce desired behaviors during paired grouping formats. However, there are several advantages. First, children have always learned a great deal from their peers. Second, the utilization of paired partnerships, in which there is a clear focus, can provide additional support with reading and learning for all students. Overall, when systematic training is provided, pairs have the potential to be an integral and useful component of any classroom reading program.

The teacher must model, foster, and reinforce desired behaviors during paired grouping formats.

7

Wee Readers: Reading Workshop in Kindergarten

Gloria Harter's Classroom

GLORIA HARTER TEACHES AT-RISK KINDERGARTEN CHILDREN in the Bright Beginnings Program in Oshkosh, Wisconsin. The children are identified by a screening battery as performing behind their expected age levels in the areas of language development, auditory skills, or visual skills. In this extended-day kindergarten program, the classes are limited to fifteen or fewer students, with a full-time teacher and a teaching assistant. The children receive a variety of learning experiences in a variety of grouping formats, including whole-group instruction, small-group instruction, learning centers, and free-choice activities.

Gloria began experimenting with the reading workshop model to see if it could be a valuable tool for providing alternative grouping formats for reading instruction in kindergarten. Her objective was to create an atmosphere in which kindergarten children would begin to see themselves as contributing members of the reading society. That society consisted of their teacher and classmates as well as each of them individually.

Like Frank Smith (1988), Gloria believes that students must view themselves as members of the literacy club. With this thought in mind, Gloria developed a membership card for the Wee Readers Club (see Figure 7-1). The children receive this card after sharing a book with the class for the first time, and they keep the card in the folder that houses their daily journal and Wee Readers Log. The club reminds all students, even those who might be struggling a bit, that they are all members of the community of readers. The program

> The Wee Readers Club reminds all students, even those who are struggling, that they are all members of the community of readers.

55

Figure 7-1. Membership Card for the Wee Readers Club (Adapted from Gloria Harter, Oshkosh, WI)

avoids sorting and labeling young children in the detrimental way that makes some students begin to see themselves as outsiders to the literacy club.

One concern that Gloria had was adapting the reading workshop model so it would be developmentally appropriate for the kindergarten child. The changes she made in the reading workshop format are reflected in Figure 7-2. Each part of her cycle will be discussed next.

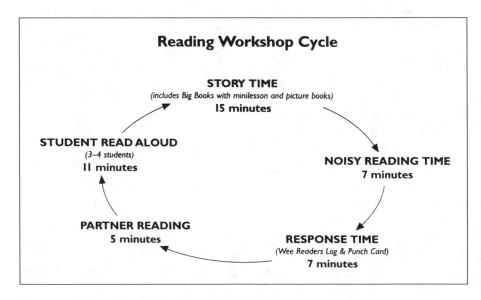

Figure 7-2. Adapted from Gloria Harter, Oshkosh, WI

Story Time

The story time segment of Wee Readers is a combination of teacher-read literature, Big Book shared reading, poetry reading, sing alongs of favorite songs placed on sentence strips, and minilessons. As discussed in Chapter 4, minilessons are short instructional lessons often referred to as focus lessons. Gloria's minilessons usually deal with identification of rhyming words or words repeated throughout a text. Story Time is structured as a large-group activity, but the objective during this time is still to encourage active involvement of the students during the literature experience. Gloria often asks the children to help her read the story by filling in rhyming words, "reading" the repetitive parts, or predicting what might happen next.

Noisy Reading Time

Noisy Reading Time is the kindergarten version of sustained silent reading. It is noisy because the children are reading aloud the texts they have memorized, sharing thoughts with each other concerning pictures, and sometimes listening to tapes of favorite stories. Noisy Reading Time is structured as an individual activity, though students often pair up during this time. During this time, one student joins Gloria on the teacher's chair so that she can read aloud the child's selection. Usually there are two or three additional students who choose to listen. The child sharing his or her selection with Gloria is often the child whose turn it is to share that day during Student Read-Aloud. Reading the selection aloud with the student guarantees that the child is indeed familiar with the story before he or she is asked to share it with the group.

Response Time

Response Time is structured as a large-group activity even though each student is working individually. The response time segment in Wee Readers has two parts. First, each child records the selection in his or her Wee Readers Log. The child records the date, the title of the story, and a brief sketch to illustrate a favorite part of the story. The child indicates whether he or she liked the story by drawing a happy or sad face or circling *yes* or *no*. The child then records who might like to read the story next. During this period, Gloria walks around assisting children with their log entry. She gives help to those

Figure 7-3. Wee Readers Punch Card (Adapted from Gloria Harter, Oshkosh, WI)

who need assistance in recording the title, and she encourages them to draw a picture that tells about the story.

The second part of response time is the punch card (see Figure 7-3). Gloria designed this punch card to help children experience different kinds of books. The punch card is divided into eight classifications: magazines, fairy tales, ABC books, counting books, animal stories, stories about children, rhyming books, and big books. Each of the eight sections has four dots, which Gloria will punch out with a hole puncher. Part of the responsibility of each child is to determine which kind of book he or she chose. As the card fills up, the child must be aware of which sections are no longer available as a choice during Noisy Reading Time.

Partner Reading

As the children finish their entries in the Wee Readers Log, they are encouraged to find a partner to read with until all students are finished. This is the Partner Reading segment of Wee Readers and takes place back in the reading corner. The teacher's role at this point is to encourage the children to share with a partner and to continue to stay involved with their selection.

Student Read-Aloud

The final segment is Student Read-Aloud. At this time, the class has moved back to a large-group format. Several students come to the teacher's chair to read their books to the class. Each student basically retells the story. If the story is unknown to the student, he or she "reads" the pictures. When the student finishes telling the story, the student indicates whether he or she liked the book by holding up a stick puppet that has a happy face on one side and a sad face on the other side. This is a review of information that the student has already recorded in the Wee Readers Log.

Adaptations to Wee Readers

Initially Gloria chose to block out forty-five minutes for the entire cycle, but after implementing the program, she decided this was too long for beginning kindergartners. In the fall, she now limits the time allotted for Wee Readers to thirty minutes. Kindergarten children will stay engaged if the total time is limited to thirty minutes and involves a number of different activities (minilesson, noisy reading, response, and sharing).

Another adaptation Gloria made involved limiting the number of children who share during Student Read-Aloud to one per day. She believes it is important to give each child more time to share his or her story in order to instill confidence, instead of rushing through each child's sharing.

> **It is important to give each child adequate time to share his or her story in order to instill confidence.**

The Wee Readers Program has continued to evolve. As Gloria observed which segments the children enjoyed and which were difficult for them, she found that Story Time needed to be limited to two experiences at the most. Now she reads one or two selections of literature or one story and a Big Book with a minilesson. At other times during the day, the class reads poetry and songs written on sentence strips, usually as a transition activity to gather the children together. Another discovery was that the minilessons that pertain to word recognition or beginning sounds are more effective apart from the Wee Readers cycle. The minilessons at Story Time are now related to following story sequence, attending to details, and predicting outcomes.

Another segment that needed revision was Partner Reading. By the time the children had listened to stories, participated in Noisy Reading Time, and logged their selections, they were less willing to read to a partner. Also, during Noisy Reading Time, the students often paired up to enjoy a book with a friend. With this in mind, Gloria saw less need for Partner Reading within the cycle.

In order to keep this activity developmentally appropriate for each kindergarten student, Gloria found it necessary to use oral response as a transition to the written log. Some children were less ready to log their experiences in a written format. For these children, it was necessary for an adult to take dictation from the child and write the response in the log. Gradually the child assumed the responsibility for writing in the log. The adult could write the book title and the name of the classmate who might like to read it next. The child could sketch a favorite part or just let the title of the story be the record. Most children were agreeable to drawing a happy face or a sad face to indicate whether or not they enjoyed the book. To maintain each child's interest in and enthusiasm for reading, it is important to keep the response oral for the children who need that format.

One addition to the log was a list with the date and title of each book read in the last quarter of the year. This list, along with a copy of one page from the Wee Readers Log, is put in the child's portfolio for review by other teachers the child works with.

As Gloria has continued to use Wee Readers as a tool to create the atmosphere of a reading society within her classroom, the cycle has become more consistent. Now she lets the natural reactions of the children drive the process. Figure 7-4 shows the cycle as implemented in the fall. In the second semester, the students begin to log their reading into their Wee Readers Logs. Figure 7-5 shows what the cycle looks like during the spring semester.

In addition to Wee Readers, the children participate in other literacy activities, including Wee Writers (the daily journal), daily news, word searches,

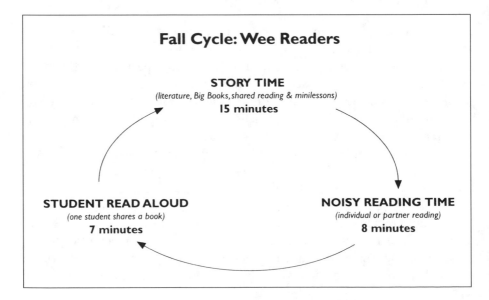

Figure 7-4. Adapted from Gloria Harter, Oshkosh, WI

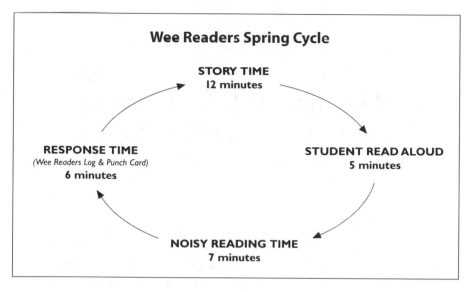

Figure 7-5. Adapted from Gloria Harter, Oshkosh, WI

and reading/writing the room. Wee Writers is the first activity of the day, as the children write in daily journals on a topic they choose. Daily news is a one- or two-sentence news story the class composes together about family or school activities. After the story is recorded on chart paper, the children volunteer to participate in a word search by drawing a circle around any word they can read. As well, the children read or write the room by going around reading and/or copying any environmental print that they are aware of in the room. This may include labels on furniture, a monthly mural that illustrates a poem or song appropriate for the month, and various bulletin boards. One bulletin board is designated as a word board that has illustrations and labels important to the month.

The Wee Readers Club is an important part of improving the children's communication skills and helping them enter a literate society. By the end of their kindergarten year, the students enjoy listening to stories and participating in shared reading. They are active readers during Noisy Reading Time and are able to log their reading selections according to their developmental level. They are willing to share stories with friends. They have benefited from a variety of reading activities in a variety of grouping formats. Overall, Gloria's students have experienced success as members of the Wee Readers Club, and she intends to continue increasing the club's membership in the future.

8

Reading Workshop for the First-Grade Emergent Reader

Brenda Wallace's Classroom

WHILE FIRST-GRADE TEACHERS ARE USED TO ENCOUNTERING A variety of student abilities, the challenge of instructing these varied individuals is often new. Teachers must constantly evolve in their efforts to meet the students' diverse needs. When Brenda Wallace, a first-grade teacher, began using an approach to teaching reading that was influenced by the whole language philosophy, she was excited to see the ability groups disappear and a community of readers replace them. As she observed her reading community, however, it became evident that not all children were equally excited about the whole-group instruction around the patterned, predictable Big Book for the day. She became concerned that as the class worked as a whole to learn emergent reading strategies, she was not meeting the needs of her advanced readers. At that time, she began searching for a flexible grouping format to meet her students' varied reading abilities.

> **Teachers must constantly evolve in their efforts to meet the students' diverse needs.**

In contrast, writing instruction in Brenda's classroom took place on an individual basis at each child's developmental level. She found that implementation of writers' workshop was very successful in first grade. It became natural to teach writing strategies using literature and material taken from the students' writing. The most appropriate time for this instruction was prior to a sustained writing time, and the children enjoyed and asked for writers' workshop during the day. They were proud to see their writing improve.

This experience led Brenda to wonder if reading could be taught using the same method. Since the children's writing improved through writing practice,

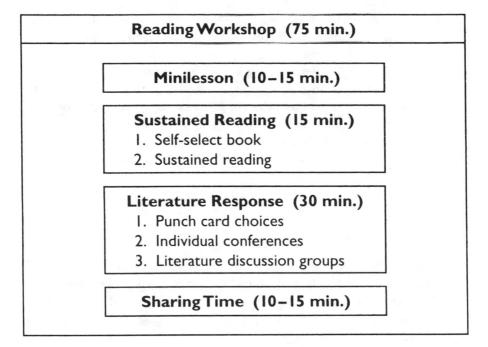

Figure 8-1. The Reading Workshop (Adapted from Reutzel and Cooter, 1991)

shouldn't their reading also improve through reading practice? Her discoveries are highlighted here.

Reading Workshop in the Classroom

Reading workshop (Atwell, 1998) provides an organization scheme for meeting the needs of individual readers. With some modifications, Brenda found it to be successful in first grade. Figure 8-1 illustrates the components of her reading workshop. During the minilesson, or focus lesson, the teacher offers instruction on a specific topic or skill. The time for sustained and uninterrupted reading increases as the year progresses.

Introducing Reading Workshop

At the start of the school year, Brenda was uncomfortable giving emergent readers the freedom to choose books. Her concern was that some book choices might not allow individual students to be engaged in useful reading practice. She wanted the sustained reading time to involve real reading, not a break in the day to flip through illustrations. To provide a framework for appropriate book choices, she implemented the focused study reading workshop (Jett-Simpson, 1991) that is organized around a theme, an author, or a unit the class is studying. Specific book titles are gathered to support the integrated study, and the students choose books from that framework. To provide success for all reading abilities, she began the focused reading workshop with wordless picture books. Although these books have no words, the pictures carry a clearly defined story line.

The following outline is a guide for introducing the workshop to emergent readers.

Day 1

Minilesson. Brenda shared *Good Dog Carl* by Alexandra Day and discussed the book with the whole class. She then briefly described the many available wordless picture books from which the students could choose.

Sustained Reading. The students selected other wordless picture books and became engaged with the literature.

Response Time. The students discussed their books with a partner.

Sharing Time. The students shared their books with the class.

Day 2

Minilesson. Brenda shared *Good Dog Carl* again, providing information about the author. She asked the following questions to help students begin thinking more critically about the book: "Why do you think the author wrote this book? What do you think she was thinking?"

Sustained Reading. The students reread the book they chose the day before to think about why the author wrote that book.

Response Time. The students wrote the title and author in their book journals (stapled unlined paper). Then they wrote or drew why the author might have written that book.

Sharing Time. The students shared their books and book journals with the class.

Day 3

Minilesson. Brenda shared *Carl Goes Shopping* by Alexandra Day and discussed her favorite part. She modeled writing about her favorite part in her teacher's book journal. (She also uses chart paper or a transparency on the overhead projector.)

Sustained Reading. The students reread previous books or chose a new title. Then they read to find their favorite part.

Response Time. In their book journals, the students drew their favorite part of the story and wrote why.

Sharing Time. The students shared their books and journals with the class.

Day 4

Minilesson. Brenda shared *Carl Goes Shopping* again and discussed why she might recommend this to a friend. She discussed the concept of advertising and modeled how to make an advertisement for the book.

Sustained Reading. The students reread books to find good advertising points.

Response Time. The students designed an advertisement to sell their book.

Sharing Time. The students shared their books and advertisements with the class.

Day 5

Minilesson. The students advertised their books to "sell" and then traded books with each other.

Sustained Reading. The students read their new book.

Response Time. The students met with the previous book "owner" and discussed why they thought the author wrote that story. They also compared their favorite parts.

Sharing Time. The students told if their partner's favorite part was the same as or different from their favorite part.

Further Developing the Reading Workshop

After the initial week of the reading workshop, Brenda introduced multiple copies of predictable, patterned stories in sets of four books per title. In the first minilesson, she briefly reviewed each book so the children could become familiar with the titles and stories. The children then chose a book from a framework of six different titles. This provided four children with the same title and lent itself very well to literature discussion groups.

In the third week, Brenda collected many different titles of books that had been previously introduced to the class during story time. She put these books into tubs with color-coded stickers. She gave children a specific colored sticker according to their reading level. After a minilesson on how to choose a book, the children chose a title from the tub with their corresponding sticker color. Each child chose from at least twenty-five books that were appropriate to their reading ability.

> **If teaching children to read is the goal, then limiting student choice to a provided framework is preferable to allowing students to choose books they cannot yet read.**

At this point, Brenda was concerned that suddenly she had moved back to ability-grouped readers. However, when children could choose any book from the classroom library, there were many emergent readers who were not engaged in real reading. If teaching children to read is the goal, then limiting student choice to a provided framework is preferable to allowing students to choose books they cannot yet read. As the year progresses, the sticker boundaries fade away. Several minilessons on selecting a book that is "easy," "just right," and "challenging" help provide strategies for students to use when choosing books.

The First-Grade Reading Workshop

This section reviews, the components of the first-grade reading workshop in Brenda's present classroom.

Minilessons

Some minilessons consist of describing procedures and routines. Other topics for minilessons are taken from students' reading needs, reading strategies, selected skills from a district curriculum guide, and introductions of new literature. The most important component of the lesson is the sharing of a literature story. Brenda begins each workshop by reading an interesting book, and she uses it as a catalyst for the minilesson objective.

Sustained Reading

According to Reutzel and Cooter (1991), the heart of the workshop is self-selected reading. During this time, students read chosen books alone, or they work through a book with a partner. Reading in the first grade does not have to be silent. This time allows students to become engaged in free reading for enjoyment.

Response Time

During this time, the class may be involved in a variety of activities. The teacher may have conferences with individuals or with a small-group literature circle. In Brenda's class, literature circles include four children who may discuss the same title or four different titles. Each child tells about their book, reads a favorite part, and asks the group for questions. If children are not working in these literature groups, they may be working with partners or working alone to respond to their reading book.

First-grade students, with their creative minds, become bored responding in a book journal every day. To alleviate this, Brenda implemented book response cards, which "visually remind students of their different response options and encourage them to try a variety of those options" (Ford and Larson, 1991, 2). These might include acting out the book or illustrating a poster to sell the book to others. After students have completed a book, they may choose a project idea from their response card. Brenda gives each student a card with suggestions of projects they may choose to do.

After completing a project, the student punches a hole in the corresponding project space. This tool is extremely successful and motivating. The interest becomes so high that the children begin inventing their own response ideas. Brenda then devotes minilessons to letting the students contribute ideas to develop a new task card to replace the completed original.

Sharing Time

At a daily closing time, the class comes together to share books, journals, or projects. This is an important time because it helps build a community of learners who can celebrate each other's accomplishments. Five students have a specific day each week for their sharing time. This allows each child to have the opportunity to share their success once a week.

Conclusion

As Brenda uses reading workshop in first grade, she is continuously reflecting on the value of this approach for emergent readers. We know the method is successful in the upper grades, but those students have had previous direct instruction in reading skills. For first-grade teachers, questions surface: Where does phonics fit into the workshop? What of the imposed district curriculum? When does guided reading instruction take place? What about using traditional reading groups so children are reading at their instructional level?

As Brenda reflects upon the components of reading workshop, she can find a place for direct instruction in reading. She teaches phonics and district curriculum skills in the minilessons. The literature groups provide an opportunity for guided reading lessons at students' instructional levels. The response time allows students to become active readers who interact with texts as well as with other readers. The sustained reading time provides students with the opportunity to apply their learned reading skills and strategies to real reading situations. The sharing time provides much more than any traditional reading approach could: it allows the children to feel good about themselves and their reading. They view themselves as readers in a community where they belong, not where they are in the low reading group. The children's enjoyment, confidence, and active involvement with literature are more important to Brenda than any skill they could master on a worksheet. Most important, students with emergent skills and advanced skills all demonstrate the characteristics of lifelong readers.

> **Sharing time provides much more than any traditional reading approach could: it allows the children to feel good about themselves and their reading.**

9

Reading Workshop in a Multiage Classroom

Marsha Winship's Classroom

HOW DOES A TEACHER APPROACH READING INSTRUCTION IN A multiage setting? The challenge in creating and sustaining a multiage classroom is making certain that meaningful and appropriate instruction is provided for *all* students. Since no two students go about any task in exactly the same way, it is necessary to modify and adapt instruction to include a variety of grouping formats. For Marsha Winship, the challenge was a classroom of eight-, nine-, and ten-year-olds who demonstrated a wide range of literacy development.

> The challenge in creating and sustaining a multiage classroom is making certain that meaningful and appropriate instruction is provided for *all* students.

An Informal Reading Inventory

At the beginning of each school year, Marsha administers an informal reading inventory. Informal reading inventories are composed of passages at different grade levels. During a conference with the teacher, the students read a passage selected by the teacher, retell its contents, and/or answer questions. If the students read orally, the teacher records word pronunciation errors to arrive at a score for word identification. From the information that Marsha obtains through these inventories, she can estimate a student's level of reading development and know which materials and instructional activities to provide (O'Donnell and Wood, 1992).

An informal reading inventory is just one way to obtain information. It serves as a starting point for developing understanding about a student's reading progress. Marsha also pays close attention to the books a student chooses to read, his or her attitudes about reading, and comments made during activities such as literature discussions and journal responses.

Reading Workshop

Independent Reading

It's Monday afternoon at one o'clock. This is a time of the day the class eagerly anticipates. They move toward their round tables, where four or five students sit and work together as a group. Everyone has a reading folder with pockets that contains a daily reading log, a sheet of paper to record monthly book projects, and the book the student is currently reading. This type of organization means that students rarely misplace books, and no one loses time going back to a locker to fetch the forgotten book. Each student also has a journal for responding to books, self-evaluating progress, asking questions, and any number of things related to the workshop. Marsha had moved the folders from their shelf to the tables while the students were at lunch.

The children open their folders and take out their books. For the next thirty minutes, they read silently with no interruptions. This is the beginning and the heart of reading workshop, which takes place daily, typically in a ninety-minute block. It is an enjoyable and uninterrupted time for students to connect with a text. To signal the end of independent reading time, Marsha simply turns out the lights.

Book Access and Book Choice

One of the first things students and visitors notice in Marsha's classroom are the colorful baskets filled with books, which are arranged pleasingly on the shelves that surround the outer areas of the room. Students are drawn to books displayed in an attractive manner, and the baskets allow Marsha to categorize books by genre, author, and themes. Students self-select the books they read. Periodically, a few will choose to read the same book and form a "book group." Several times during the year, the class will focus on the works of a particular author or read and discuss books pertaining to a central theme. On other occasions, they all read the same book together. Since all grouping alternatives provide different

> **Students are drawn to books displayed in an attractive manner.**

outcomes, Marsha's reading program will sometimes involve the use of one title for all students, sets of titles for small groups, and different titles for different students.

Minilessons

Marsha also teaches minilessons, or focus lessons, daily. These short instructional segments revolve around procedural issues such as the use of reading logs and journals, or student responsibilities during the reading workshop. They also revolve around elements common to all pieces of literature. Marsha presents reading strategies and skills in these minilessons.

One of the first minilessons Marsha teaches deals with making sure that students know how to choose appropriate books for themselves. As a group, they define the guidelines to use to choose books. Marsha records what the students say on big chart paper. This chart serves as a daily reminder and a handy review for students:

1. Look at the front and back cover. Read what they say.
2. Read a few pages and look at the illustrations.
3. Do the five-finger check, but try it in a couple of places. (The five-finger check is a strategy used to check the difficulty of the book. Students are taught to read a page putting down one finger for each word they miss on a page. If the student puts down all five fingers, they know the book might be too difficult.)
4. Ask a friend for a recommendation!
5. Go to a favorite author.
6. Go to the baskets and look at the labels.
7. Reread an "old favorite."

The Reading Log

After independent reading is over, students enter the pages read in their reading log. This becomes a daily and automatic habit, because one of their daily responsibilities is to keep track of their reading. Using a form on the overhead projector, Marsha also keeps track of her reading to model the use and importance of the reading log.

At different times during the year, the students are invited to look back in the log to review the pages and books they have read. The log is evidence of their progress in reading. Students have a ready list of favorite authors, the number of books read in each grading period, a record of the time it took them to read the books, and a sense of accomplishment.

Reading Response Journals

Once or twice a week, students write in their reading response journals. They write about what they are reading and how they feel about what they are reading. Students read very different materials based on individual interests and ability. It is not important for them all to read the same page of the same passage at the same time; it is important for them all to enjoy and demonstrate understanding of their reading. All of the students show through their response journals that they comprehend what they are reading.

> **It is not important for all students to read the same page of the same passage at the same time; it is important for all students to enjoy and demonstrate understanding of their reading.**

Since students are reading a variety of materials, Marsha periodically gives the class a specific question to respond to that deals with a common story element. It may be about the character, the setting, or an element of plot. Even though they are reading different books, the students can discuss a common story element. As well, hearing others talk about their books sparks students' interest and then makes them want to read the books.

Marsha also uses response journals to gain insights into students' needs concerning reading workshop. Once a month, she asks the students to evaluate the reading time. Questions include: What's going well? What do you need more of? What do you need less of? Is there something we need to discuss and change? Response journals help Marsha reflect on her instruction and its effectiveness.

Individual Conferences

By working with a parent volunteer and support staff, Marsha is able to meet weekly with each student so they can read aloud and discuss the book being read. The talk is natural. Questions are asked out of curiosity, not out of a teacher's manual.

Individual conferences allow teachers to listen to a student's interpretation and personal opinion of a book. It also serves as a way to gain insight into the student's reading process. Students are asked to be ready to read a page or so from the book. This is a time for teachers to take notes, record reading strategies used, and note any miscues.

Marsha's class also meets together weekly in small groups of four or five and as a whole class to talk about what they are reading. As in the journals, Marsha sometimes focuses talk on a particular story element. Discussions often move beyond talk about the literature being read, as they involve every aspect of teaching and learning. For example, they discuss what to do when they come to a word they do not know or how to make sure they are understanding what they are reading. As students share their strategies, Marsha often records what they say on chart paper. She hangs the charts on the wall, where they serve as handy resources. As students discuss these issues, they begin to understand that all readers encounter the same problems, and they continue to offer each other support and solutions.

Literary Extension Activities

Literary extension activities are projects combined with oral presentations that take the place of worksheets. About once a month, students choose a book they have read to share with the class. There are many options for projects. For example, they can present Venn diagrams that compare and contrast two books, or they can construct a chart of the main story elements of a book. Students can tape a discussion on a book with a peer who has read the same book, or give a booktalk on several books by one author.

In the beginning, many of these projects are modeled so that students have a better understanding of the expectations. Usually the class begins with the same project and, as the students become familiar with several options, they begin to create their own original versions. These activities are fun and motivational. They extend the students' appreciation and understanding of a story. They also reinforce the development and integration of reading, writing, speaking, and thinking.

Assessing Individual Progress

It is the teacher's job to document students' literacy development. Many sources of data can be used, including the informal reading inventory previously described, literature logs, reading journals, conference notes, student comments during discussions, running records of students' miscues or word pronunciation errors, and summary sheets. Interviews, written responses by students, pictures of projects, and quarterly self-evaluations in which students set personal goals all provide valuable information.

In Marsha's classroom, assessment is ongoing and closely reflects the classroom instruction. Each child decides what is successful about his or her work, what he or she can do to improve, and what changes can be made to enhance progress. Because the literacy acquisition of individual students varies, Marsha does not define the same expected outcome for all students. However, she expects each student to make continuous progress at acquiring literacy.

Assessment needs to be ongoing. It should closely reflect the classroom instruction.

Beyond two scheduled parent conferences, Marsha arranges several informal meetings with families to share assessment procedures and the purpose of portfolios. Several times a year, she invites families to participate in the reading workshop. Going through a day with their child gives family members a better understanding of what happens at school.

Summary of Reading Workshop Activities

The following list summarizes major instructional activities that take place in reading workshop:

1. Students keep simple records of books they are reading in a daily reading log.
2. Students share reactions to reading through book talks, discussions, and writing activities in their reading response journals.
3. The teacher conducts periodic conferences with individual students to discuss impressions, assess comprehension, monitor reading progress, and stimulate further reading.
4. Students create monthly literacy projects to share with peers. This serves to extend their appreciation and understanding of favorite books.

Besides these elements, there are several things that teachers can do to ensure students' success as readers. These include understanding the stages of reading development, providing appropriate instruction, understanding grouping alternatives, and combining a workshop approach with a positive learning environment.

10

Grouping Without Tracking: Whole-Class Instruction in Second Grade

Michael Ford's Classroom

THERE ARE TIMES WHEN TEACHERS DECIDE THAT ALL OF THEIR students should read the same book. Reasons may range from seeking convenience to creating community. How can teachers use the same text in a class of students with different reading abilities? What is the best way to use a whole-class text so that students who can operate independently are allowed to do so, while those who need support receive it? The task is quite challenging. Such was the case when Michael Ford was asked to model flexible grouping in a second-grade classroom during a residency with the Fort Atkinson School District in Wisconsin. The book was William Steig's *Brave Irene,* a story with an enjoyable narrative and theme of perseverance. Since the class was going to build future reading instruction based on this book, it was decided to use the book as a common core selection for all students.

Michael realized that this book would be very challenging for some students in this second-grade classroom. Grouping Without Tracking (Paratore, 1990) is one possible way to accomplish this goal. Like many whole-class models, students work together when preparing for and responding to the reading of the text. When actually reading the text, students are grouped according to ability. Michael has used this model in a number of classroom settings. It may be best illustrated with the lesson described in this chapter.

Frontloading the Reading Lesson

Most teachers know the importance of prereading activities, but the front end of the reading lesson becomes even more critical when asking a group

Box One What do all these words have in common?	Box Two Tell about a time when you were brave in winter.	Box Three Predict what the story will be about.
Box Four Adjust your prediction based on these new story words.	Box Five Listen and check your prediction.	Box Six At the end, rate how well you worked.

Figure 10-1. Six Box Grid Worksheet

of diverse readers to read the same book. As they read, able readers naturally invoke all the strategies that they have internalized. Less able readers often do not. The gap between the two groups of readers widens unless teachers effectively frontload the reading lesson.

> **The front end of the reading lesson becomes even more critical when asking a group of diverse readers to read the same book.**

Prior to the frontloading activities for *Brave Irene*, Michael gave each student a grid worksheet containing six boxes (see Figure 10-1). This worksheet provided small spaces for students to record responses in a low-risk manner during the whole-group activities. It was designed to keep more students engaged and to provide part of a paper trail that would be collected and assessed at the end of the lesson.

The class began the lesson by looking at six phrases containing some difficult vocabulary words from the first part of the story. Michael placed these phrases on an overhead transparency and invited the students to echo them after he said them. Then the class chanted the list of phrases together. Next, Michael asked students to activate their own background knowledge. Using convergent thinking skills, they wrote a word or phrase in box number one that reminded them of the words on the overhead. They shared with their neighbors before deciding as a class that the phrases all related to winter storms.

Using divergent thinking, the students tapped their background knowledge a bit more by turning their grids over and writing other words they knew that reminded them of winter. They shared these lists with neighbors before the class constructed a word map together. With Michael's guidance, they made a poster webbing words related to winter and looking for words in three key categories: clothing, weather, and movement. This allowed Michael to assist the students in connecting difficult words and phrases they would encounter in the story to words and phrases they already knew.

With background knowledge both developed and activated, and vocabulary in place, Michael asked the students to think more directly about the topic of the story: bravery during winter. Using an overhead grid that resembled the students' grid, Michael wrote a brief story about a time when he was brave during the winter. After modeling, he invited the students to do the same in box number two on their grids. Students first shared with their neighbors; then the class shared in the large group. Michael reminded students that the ideas they wrote down could be developed into stories like the one they were going to read. This suggestion provided a natural way for students to respond when they had some independent work time during the whole-class lesson.

In box number three, Michael asked the students to do what good readers often do: think about the book's title and make a prediction about what they thought would happen in the story. He revealed that the story was *Brave Irene* and that it was about a girl who was brave in the winter. Students immediately began to make predictions. Michael asked those familiar with the story not to reveal the events but to help him check whether predictions were close. Once predictions were shared, he placed a few more words from the story on the overhead. These words provided clues about characters and events. After practicing these words, students were allowed to revise their predictions in box number four. As students shared in the large group, the class was able to discuss the vocabulary words in the context of their predictions.

Releasing the Story

If the teacher has done an effective job frontloading, reading the story will be easier for more students. By gradually releasing responsibility for reading, understanding, and responding to the text, the teacher can guarantee that more learners in the class will also have success. With *Brave Irene*, Michael took responsibility for reading aloud the first page of the text. He placed the book behind a folder cover to conceal the illustrations and invited students to listen to the language and visualize the scene in their heads. He also asked them to check whether their predictions needed to be revised. After he was done reading, they wrote an evaluation of their prediction in box number five.

By gradually releasing responsibility for reading, understanding, and responding to the text, the teacher can guarantee that more learners in the class will also have success.

For the next part of the story, Michael put the text on an overhead transparency. The class chorally read this part. By using a text cover and gradually revealing the text on the overhead, Michael could keep all students reading together at a reasonable pace. Since the section had dialogue between Irene and her mother, Michael color-coded the lines of dialogue. Groups of students read Irene's part and others read her mother's part. Some students read the narration along with Michael. Trading parts in this simple readers' theater format was an enjoyable and low-risk way for all students to read this part of the story. By now the students were familiar with the story, content, and style. They were ready to take over the reading task.

Engaging Readers

Since Michael's goal was to promote independent and strategic readers, he wanted to let students who could read and respond to the text do so on their own. He decided to provide a simple engagement structure to their independent work to ensure that they would do this. He gave each student a fourpart story wheel (see Figure 10-2). In part one, the class worked together to draw a picture of what had happened so far in the story. Then Michael gave students clear directions to read to a certain page, stop, and draw three more times in order to fill out the story wheel. At the end of the reading for the day, the students were asked to turn their story wheels over and draw a prediction of what they thought would happen next. If students completed their work, they knew they could read their SSR books, write in their journals (perhaps a brave winter story of their own suggested by what they wrote in box number two), or share what they had read and created with a buddy.

Providing Support

Since this was a class of diverse learners, Michael also knew that some of the students would only be able to read and respond to this text with support. Since he had worked very hard to get most of the students engaged in working on their own, he was now able to form a small group of students for whom he could guide the reading of *Brave Irene* and the completion of the story wheel. In this more manageable small-group setting, he was able to provide a homogenous group of students with some additional review and skill activities not needed by all. He could guide their reading of the text by letting them listen to him,

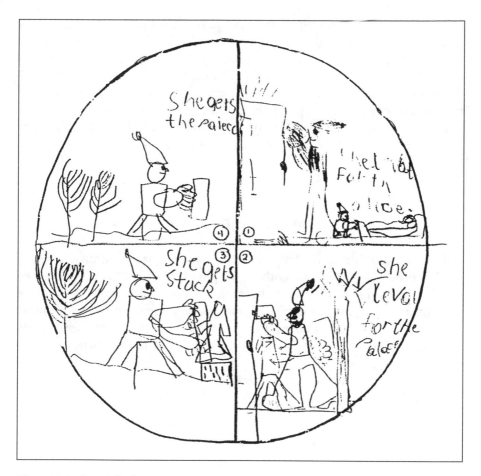

Figure 10-2. Story Wheel

read with him, echo his reading, read as a group, or, when appropriate, read on their own. They could stop along the way, and Michael could support them as they filled in their story wheels. By receiving the support they needed, they were given access to the same instruction provided to the more able readers.

Responding as a Whole Class

The response activity provides another opportunity to bring the class together as a whole. If the teacher has done an effective job of supporting the less able readers, they should feel comfortable contributing to the response activity since they have successfully accessed the text. With *Brave Irene,* the class continued to practice the visualization strategies used in the individual story wheels by creating a whole-class story wheel. Michael divided the class into seven heterogeneously grouped teams and gave each team a segment of the circle and a piece of the story. Each team had to reread their text and draw an illustration to go with that part of the story. When completed, the circle segments were sequenced on a poster. Each team wrote a one-sentence summary of their scene, which Michael attached, thus adding a little print to the story wheel. Michael ended the lesson by asking students to self-evaluate their work habits for the lesson in box number six of their grids.

Other Considerations

The Grouping Without Tracking model needs to be placed within a balanced literacy program that includes other grouping formats. If the model is used exclusively, its disadvantages will become magnified. The support group of students may become too static and not receive enough practice with more appropriate texts. Other students may not receive enough teacher interaction and may desire more challenging texts. But when a teacher believes that a certain text should be experienced by all students in a classroom of diverse abilities, the Grouping Without Tracking model offers a workable way to effectively achieve that goal.

11

Flexible Grouping
in Middle School

Mary Rae Johnson's Classroom

THE CLASS MARY RAE TEACHES IN MIDDLE SCHOOL IS OFFICIALLY
titled Communication Arts. The purpose of the class is to integrate the language arts and include reading, writing, listening, and speaking. Reading workshop and writers' workshop provide the framework for the class. Within this
framework, she uses flexible grouping for a variety of language arts activities.
Different circumstances determine how she organizes her flexible groups. She
forms flexible groups on the basis of ability, need, chance, choice, or interest.
The flexible groups in the classroom are temporary. The groupings do not last
for long periods of time nor are they static.

Mary Rae taught for many years when ability grouping was the most
common form of instruction. She found it very frustrating. She has discovered
that her heterogeneous groups are a wonderful improvement. While there are
circumstances when she feels compelled to organize her groups based on the
students' ability to perform a certain strategy or task, students also benefit
from other grouping formats.

Ability or Need Grouping

Learning how to write effective buddy letters is one instance where Mary Rae
often forms flexible groups based upon student need. Her eighth graders self-
select the books they read, and then they are required to write buddy letters
to each other about these books. About the fourth week of school, Mary Rae
models a buddy letter on the overhead. She shares the kind of information and
thoughts that should be in an effective buddy letter. She then gives students a

copy of the grading criteria and asks them to write a buddy letter to the teacher. During the next class period, the students exchange these buddy letters and utilize the grading criteria to establish a grade for each other's letters. The students circle the aspects of the buddy letter that fit the grading criteria.

After these initial lessons, Mary Rae assigns students to a buddy. Every other week, she expects them to have a conversation in writing about their two books. If some students experience difficulties writing buddy letters that meet the established criteria, she groups these students and assists them with their letter writing. To do so, she models another buddy letter, and the group discusses exactly what they need to do to meet the criteria. This group meets only one or two class periods unless otherwise indicated by the students' progress.

As well, the class may have several short-term review sessions as the year progresses for students who are still experiencing difficulty. In most cases, Mary Rae leaves involvement in the review lesson up to the students. They can choose to attend or not attend. At times, however, students who need the most help often do not recognize that fact. When this occurs, Mary Rae requires students to be present. If a student who is already doing well also decides to join a review session, she allows that student to attend.

During writers' workshop, Mary Rae also forms flexible groups according to skills the students have not mastered. She evaluates their stories or essays, and when a specific strategy or skill seems to be causing difficulties, she groups students according to their need. For example, there may be students who still have trouble organizing their writing into paragraphs. She meets with them and uses their writing to help them decide when to begin a new paragraph. She might also call together a group of students who are having trouble writing dialogue that is believable and mechanically correct. At times, she has organized groups of students who need help with homonyms, spelling strategies, or punctuation. These groupings are usually very short-term and, in most cases, voluntary.

> **When a specific strategy or skill seems to be causing difficulties, teachers should group students according to their need.**

Chance Grouping

Chance grouping occurs when Mary Rae arranges seating charts. Students in the classroom are seated at round tables, with three or four students at a table. These table groups engage in a variety of group activities during writers' workshop and reading workshop.

When arranging seating charts, Mary Rae tries to accomplish a variety of things. First of all, she separates any students who encourage each other to be disruptive or distracting. As well, she finds it beneficial to purposefully integrate the sexes. Most of the male-female relationships in eighth grade revolve around "going together." She wants the students to establish and experience male-female relationships that are based upon the sharing of thoughts, knowledge, ideas, and opinions. She rearranges these chance-seating arrangements about eight times a year and tries to avoid the same combinations of students if possible.

Mary Rae also believes students need to be able to work cooperatively, and many of the class activities encourage or require cooperative or collaborative behavior. In reading workshop, students self-select their books. During group sharing, they share something about their particular book. For example, when Mary Rae teaches her students about good story leads, she covers the idea from a reader's perspective and a writer's perspective. First, she shares some excellent leads from books or short stories in the classroom. Then she asks students to read the beginning of their book and decide if it is a good lead and why or why not. Once all students are prepared, she has them share the lead from their current book and their evaluation of that lead. Since the table groups are randomly selected, the variety of books being read and the types of leads vary greatly. These types of discussions encourage students to share the books they are reading and participate in book talk. Students learn about other books and become interested in reading the books of others at their table.

One of the next lessons deals with the actual writing of leads. Students are asked to write about ten leads they feel would really grab the reader. They also share these in table groups. Students are encouraged to voluntarily share with the entire class. Students gradually become a little more comfortable sharing information with a large group.

With chance grouping, there is always a good possibility that a really worthwhile discussion will happen. For example, throughout the year, students in reading workshop select a short passage from the book they are reading to read to their table group. Students must justify their choices. At one session, Mary Rae was a group member at a table where a student read a selection from *Pinballs* by Betsy Byars. She chose the section in which Harvey's father accidentally ran over Harvey's legs and what should have been the happiest day of Harvey's life became the worst. The student's comment was, "I think I like this part because I can relate to important days being ruined." What followed was a very interesting discussion about some truly horrible days.

> With chance grouping, there is always a good possibility that a really worthwhile discussion will happen.

Choice Grouping

Choice grouping occurs quite often in Mary Rae's classroom. Many middle school students feel strongly about selecting whom they would like to work with on projects or assignments. There can be drawbacks to this selection process, and some students may feel excluded. However, with careful guidance, a teacher can involve all students in selecting peers for sharing or working together. For example, during group sharing in writers' workshop, some students are too uncomfortable sharing their writing with the entire class. It is less threatening if they share with a smaller group, especially if it is a group they have self-selected. As the year progresses and the students share their writing more, Mary Rae moves from choice grouping and assigns student groups for sharing. Eventually she requires all students to share a piece of their writing or a section of it with the entire class. In this way, they gradually work toward the type of whole-class sharing that students normally find threatening.

Interest Grouping

At times, students are grouped by interest. For example, they may work in literature circles based on their interest in a particular book.

There are three grade-level themes in Mary Rae's eighth-grade Communication Arts curriculum: relationships, suspense, and conflict. The class reads novels in which these themes are the main focus.

When the class begins a new theme, Mary Rae distributes a different novel to each table group. The groups, which are probably chance groups, read the back cover and the first few pages. They then prepare a short book talk for the whole class about their predictions of the contents of the books. As students listen to these book talks, they write down at least three titles that interest them and that they are willing to read. Students then select a book. Students who choose the same title are grouped together for discussion purposes and comprehension activities.

Students who read the same title also prepare a short skit about their book. Their purpose is to interest their audience in reading the book, and many groups succeed. Skits often range from TV talk-show formats to game shows to scenes from the book. The group earns a grade that is shared equally by all members. Many times, students read more than one book in a specific theme. Those students select the title group they want to work with for the skit. Students also have an individual project that is part of their grade.

Final Thoughts

Teaching new strategies or skills to a large heterogeneous group is how Mary Rae begins most instruction in her classroom. Once she is aware of the skills or strategies that her students need, she can begin arranging flexible groups. Some are based upon need or ability. Other grouping formats include chance, choice, and interest groups that are formed on a regular basis. All the groups are truly flexible and short-term. Throughout the year, as students are grouped in a variety of combinations, they become comfortable working as contributing members in a large group and as contributing members in a short-term flexible group.

> **When students are grouped in a variety of combinations over time, they become comfortable working as contributing members in a large group and as contributing members in a short-term flexible group.**

Appendix: Overview of Common Grouping Patterns

Type of Grouping	Description	Advantages
Whole-Class Grouping	The teacher works with the class as a whole.	Whole-class grouping allows more efficient use of teacher preparation time.
	Everyone participates in the same activity or discussion.	It provides a common knowledge base for all students.
	The same text is used for all students.	It develops a sense of the classroom community.

Cooperative Grouping	The students work together in small heterogenous groups.	The activity tends to be very focused.
	The focus of the group is to accomplish a common goal.	Because of group size and group focus, all students tend to be involved.
	Group members usually read the same text.	The teacher can address problems more easily than in a whole-group setting.
	The teacher usually assigns a grade to the group as a whole.	Students develop social interaction skills through working together.

Disadvantages	When does it work?	When doesn't it work?
Differentiation of instruction is difficult in whole-class instruction.	Whole-class grouping works when different skill levels are accounted for.	Whole-class grouping does not work if the activity or skill is too easy or too difficult for the students involved.
Lower-level students can easily get lost if not monitored carefully.	It works when everyone in the class needs the same skill, content, or experience.	It does not work if all students cannot read the text.
Higher-level students may be unchallenged.		
There is the danger of possible lack of interaction and participation by all students.		

Children do not easily cooperate.	Cooperative grouping works if every group member knows and understands the focus and task.	Cooperative grouping does not work if students do not understand the task required of them.
If interaction skills are not taught and practiced, cooperative grouping can be a disaster.	It works if the input of all group members is equally important and equally valued.	It does not work if the task involves lower-level skill-and-drill practice.
The teacher can lose control unless the group clearly understands the focus and task.	It works if students are taught interaction skills and how to cooperate.	It does not work if the group is set up as a tutorial.
Group grades are often misunderstood by both students and parents.	It works if the group is involved in higher-level thinking activities.	

Type of Grouping	Description	Advantages
Collaborative Grouping	Students work together to share their reading or complete an activity.	A small group allows individuals to have more input and be more interactive.
	They may read the same or different texts.	Small-group sharing can be more focused than sharing done in a large group.
	The teacher evaluates each student individually.	Collaborative groups allow for a stronger emphasis upon student choice.
	Literature study groups or literature circles can be a form of collaborative grouping.	

Interest Grouping	Students work in small groups based upon their interest in the topic, activity, or text.	Interest grouping increases student motivation because the group activity is based upon student choice.
	Students usually read the same text or texts, which are related to the shared interest of the group.	Small groups tend to be more focused than large groups.
	Literature study groups or literature circles can be a form of interest grouping, as can content area inquiry groups.	

Disadvantages	When does it work?	When doesn't it work?
Some students may dominate.	Collaborative grouping works well when group procedures are clearly understood.	If procedures are vague or open-ended, collaborative grouping may not be effective.
If tasks or procedures are not clearly understood, the group can easily move off task.	The activity or task should be within the capabilities of all group members.	If student interaction skills are assumed, problems may occur.
	For example, if reading is required, all members should be able to read the text.	
	Collaborative grouping works when students are guided to develop interaction skills.	

Student interests do not always reflect their needs.	Interest groupings work when all students actually share the same interests.	Interest groupings do not work when social relationships take on more important than the group work.
Some students can be left out if group composition is based upon interests they do not share.	They work when the activities designed to promote the interest are as attractive as the interest itself.	They do not work if the group activities are not attractive to the members.

Type of Grouping	Description	Advantages
Special Need or Skill Groupings	Students work in small groups based upon their reading level and/or instructional needs.	Student needs can receive direct emphasis.
	Skill and strategy development is the focus of the group.	Similarity of student need allows for a very sharp focus.
	Guided reading is a form of special need or skill grouping.	All group members can read the text.

Type of Grouping	Description	Advantages
Paired Grouping	Students pair up with another student.	Pairs can be very focused, and the relationship between the partners can be extremely rewarding.
	They read the same text in a shared format.	

Type of Grouping	Description	Advantages
Individual Work	Students read or work individually.	Individual work can be very motivating if students are allowed some measure of choice.
	All students in a classroom may read different texts.	Students can become aware of their own understanding of a task.
	Self-selected silent reading and readers' workshop are forms of individual work.	The teacher can evaluate work apart from group influences.

Disadvantages	When does it work?	When doesn't it work?
Student perceptions of such groupings can be negative.	Special need groupings work when the focus is very specific in nature and when specific instructional outcomes are targeted.	Special need groupings do not work when group membership remains static.
The same students tend to be chosen for and remain in these groups.	They work when group membership changes periodically and when these groupings experiences are balanced with others.	They do not work if they are the only form of classroom grouping used.
		They can be problematic if group membership is based upon teacher impressions of ability or general characteristics as opposed to specific assessment data.

If a problem arises, there is a lack of group input.	Pairs work if the partners are socially matched.	Pairs do not work if the partners are at very different skill levels.
One partner can become too reliant upon the other or too responsible for the other.	They work if students have input into choice of partners.	They do not work if the partners are uncomfortable with one another.
	They work if both partners are equally skilled or if one is slightly more able than the other.	

The teacher may not be able to attend to individual needs when they occur.	Individual work is effective if the activity or text is at an appropriate level and if the procedures are clearly understood by the student.	Individual work is not effective if the work is too easy or difficult or if the procedures are unclear.
Some students become disengaged when working independently, especially if the work is not appropriate to their level.	It is effective if the student understands the purpose or value of the activity.	It is not effective if the student does not understand the purpose and value of the activity.

References

Allington, R. L. 1980. "Teacher Interruption Behavior During Primary Grade Oral Reading." *Journal of Educational Psychology,* 72, 371–374.

———. 1983a. "The Reading Instruction Provided Readers of Differing Reading Abilities." *The Elementary School Journal,* 83, 548–559.

———. 1983b. "Fluency: The Neglected Reading Goal." *The Reading Teacher,* 36, 656–661.

———. 1984. "Content Coverage and Contextual Reading in Reading Groups." *Journal of Reading Behavior,* 16, 85–96.

———. 2001. *What Really Matters for Struggling Readers: Designing Research-based Programs.* New York: Longman.

Allington, R., and A. McGill-Franzen. 1989a. "Different Programs, Indifferent Instruction." In *Beyond Separate Education: Quality Education for All,* edited by D. K. Lipsky and A. Gartner. Baltimore: Paul H. Brooks, 75–98.

———. 1989b. "School Response to Reading Failure: Instruction for Chapter 1 and Special Education Students in Grades Two, Four, and Eight." *The Elementary School Journal,* 89, 529–542.

Alpert, J. L. 1975. "Do Teachers Adapt Methods and Materials to Ability Groups in Reading?" *California Journal of Educational Research,* 26, 120–123.

Alvermann, D., and D. Dillon. 1991. "Ways of Knowing Are Ways of Seeking." *Reading Research Quarterly,* 26, 329–333.

Alvermann, D. D., and D. W. Moore. 1991. "Secondary School Reading." In *Handbook of Reading Research, Vol. II,* edited by R. Barr, M. L. Kamil, P. Mosenthal, and P. D. Pearson. New York: Longman, 951–983.

Anderson, R. C., E. H. Hiebert, J. A. Scott, and I. Wilkinson. 1985. *Becoming a Nation of Readers.* Washington, DC: National Institute of Education.

Aronson, E. 1978. *The Jigsaw.* Beverly Hills: Sage.

Atwell, N. 1998. *In the Middle: New Understandings of Writing, Reading, and Learning.* Portsmouth, NH: Boynton/Cook.

Barr, R. 1975. "How Children Are Taught to Read: Grouping and Pacing." *School Review,* 75, 479–498.

———. 1995. "What Research Says About Ability Grouping in the Past and Present and What It Suggests about the Future." In *Flexible Grouping for Literacy in the Elementary Grades,* edited by M. C. Radencich and L. J. McKay. Boston: Allyn and Bacon, 1–24.

Barr, R., and R. Dreeben. 1988. *How Schools Work.* Chicago: University of Chicago Press.

Barr, R., and R. Dreeben. 1991. "Grouping Students for Reading Instruction." In *Handbook of Reading Research, Vol. II,* edited by R. Barr, M. L. Kamil, P. Mosenthal, and P. D. Pearson. New York: Longman, 885–910.

Berghoff, B., and K. Egawa. 1991. "No More 'Rocks': Grouping to Give Students Control of their Learning." *The Reading Teacher,* 44, 535–541.

Blachowicz, C., and D. Ogle. 2001. *Reading Comprehension: Strategies for Independent Learners.* New York: Guilford.

Borko, H. 1982. "Teachers' Decision Policies about Grouping Students for Reading Instruction." In *New Inquiries in Reading Research and Instruction,* edited by J. A. Niles and L. A. Harris. Thirty-First Yearbook of the National Reading Conference. Rochester, NY: National Reading Conference, 220–226.

Brown, K. 1999–2000. "What Kind of Text—For Whom and When? Textual Scaffolding for Beginning Readers." *The Reading Teacher,* 53, 292–307.

Caldwell, J. S. 2002. *Reading Assessment: A Primer for Teachers and Tutors.* New York: Guilford.

Carver, R. P., and J. V. Hoffman. 1981. "The Effect of Practice Through Repeated Reading on Gain in Reading Ability Using a Computer-based Instructional System." *Reading Research Quarterly,* 16, 374–390.

Clay, M. 1993. *Reading Recovery: A Guidebook for Teachers in Training.* Portsmouth, NH: Heinemann.

Cunningham, P. M. 1988. "Working Together in Reading. *Reading Today,* 6, 24.

Cunningham, P. M., D. P. Hall, and M. Defee. 1991. "Non-ability Grouped Multi-level Instruction: A Year in a First Grade Classroom." *The Reading Teacher,* 44, 566–571.

Daniels, H. 2001. *Literature Circles: Voice and Choice in Book Clubs and Reading Groups.* 2nd ed. Portland, ME: Stenhouse.

Davidson, J. 1982. "The DR-TA: Avoiding Common Pitfalls." *Reading Horizons,* 23, 54–58.

DeVries, D., and R. E. Slavin. 1978. "Teams-games-tournaments (TGT): Review of Ten Classroom Experiments." *Journal of Research and Development in Education,* 12, 28–38.

Dowhower, S. L. 1987. "Effects of Repeated Readings on Second-grade Transitional Readers' Fluency and Comprehension." *Reading Research Quarterly,* 22, 389–406.

———. 1989. "Repeated Reading: Research into Practice." *The Reading Teacher,* 42, 502–507.

Dreeben, R. 1984. "First-grade Reading Groups: Their Formation and Change." In *The Social Context of Instruction,* edited by P. L. Peterson, L. C. Wilkinson, and M. Hallinan. New York: Academic, 69–84.

Durkin, D. 1978–79. "What Classroom Observations Reveal about Reading Comprehension Instruction." *Reading Research Quarterly,* 14, 481–533.

Eder, D. 1981. "Ability Grouping as a Self-fulfilling Prophecy: A Micro-analysis of Teacher-student Interaction." *Sociology of Education,* 54, 151–161.

Elbaum, B., S. W. Moody, and J. S. Schumm. 1999. "Mixed-ability Grouping for Reading: What Students Think." *Learning Disabilities Research and Practice,* 14, 61–66.

Esposito, D. 1973. "Homogeneous and Heterogeneous Ability Grouping: Principal Findings and Implications for Evaluating and Designing More Effective Educational Environments." *Review of Educational Research,* 43, 163–179.

Fawson, P., and R. Reutzel. 2000. "But I Only Have a Basal: Implementing Guided Reading in the Early Grades." *The Reading Teacher,* 55, 84–97.

Filby, N., B. Barnett, and S. Bossert. 1982. *Grouping Practices and Their Consequences.* San Francisco: Far West Laboratory for Educational Research and Development.

Ford, M., and J. Larson. 1991. "Reading Responses: It's All in the Cards." *The Whole Idea: Newsletter for Innovative Teachers,* 2, 5.

Fountas, I., and G. S. Pinnell. 1996. *Guided Reading: Good First Teaching for All Children.* Portsmouth, NH: Heinemann.

French, D., and S. Rothman. 1990. *Structuring Schools for Student Success: A Focus on Ability Grouping.* Quincy, MA: Massachusetts Board of Education.

Gambrell, L., R. Wilson, and W. Ganatt. 1981. "Classroom Observations of Task-attending Behaviors of Good and Poor Readers." *Journal of Educational Research,* 74, 400–404.

Gamoran, A. 1987. "Organization, Instruction, and the Effects of Ability Grouping: Comment on Slavin's 'Best-Evidence Synthesis.'" *Review of Educational Research,* 57, 341–345.

———. 1989. "Rank, Performance and Ability in Elementary School Grouping." *The Sociological Quarterly,* 30, 109–123.

———. 1991. "Rethinking Tracking and Ability Grouping." *Wisconsin School News,* 45, 9–14.

Gamoran, A., M. Nystrand, M. Berends, and P. C. LePore. 1995. "An Organizational Analysis of the Effects of Ability Grouping." *American Educational Research Journal,* 32, 687–715.

George, P. 1988. "Tracking and Ability Grouping: Which Way for the Middle School?" *Middle School Journal,* 20, 21–28.

Good, T., and J. Brophy. 1987. *Looking in Classrooms.* New York: Harper and Row.

Good, T. L., and S. Marshall. 1984. "Do Students Learn More in Heterogeneous or Homogeneous Groups?" In *The Social Context of Instruction,* edited by P. L. Peterson, L. C. Wilkinson, and M. Hallinan. New York: Academic, 15–38.

Goodlad, J. I. 1984. *A Place Called School: Prospect for the Future.* New York: McGraw Hill.

Goodman, Y., and A. Marek. 1996. *Retrospective Miscue Analysis: Revaluing Readers and Reading.* Katonah, NY: Richard C. Owens.

Greenslade, B. C. 1980. "Awareness and Anticipation: Utilizing the DR-TA in the Content Classroom." *Journal of Language Experiences,* 2, 21–28.

Haller, E. J., and M. Waterman. 1985. "The Criteria of Reading Group Assignments." *The Reading Teacher,* 38, 772–781.

Hallinan, M. 1984. "Summary and Implications." In *The Social Context of Instruction,* edited by P. L. Peterson, L. C. Wilkinson, and M. Hallinan. New York: Academic, 224–240.

Hansen, J. 2001. *When Writers Read.* 2nd ed. Portsmouth, NH: Heinemann.

Harp, B. 1989. "What Do We Put in Place of Ability Grouping?" *The Reading Teacher,* 42, 534–535.

Harvey S., and A. Goudvis. 2000. *Strategies that Work: Teaching Comprehension to Enhance Understanding.* York, ME: Stenhouse.

Haskins, R., T. Walden, and C. T. Ramey. 1983. "Teacher and Student Behavior in High- and Low-ability Groups." *Journal of Educational Psychology,* 75, 865–876.

Hiebert, E. 1983. "An Examination of Ability Grouping for Reading Instruction." *Reading Research Quarterly,* 18, 235–255.

Jett-Simpson, M. 1991. "Organizing the Whole Language Reading Class: Readers' Workshop and Focused Study Reading Workshop." *Wisconsin State Reading Association Journal,* 53, 44–55.

Johnson, D. W., and R. T. Johnson. 1984. "Cooperative Small Group Learning." *NASSP Curriculum Report,* 14, 1–5.

Johnson, D. W., R. T. Johnson, E. J. Holubec, and P. Roy. 1984. *Circles of Learning.* Alexandria, VA: Association for Supervision and Curriculum Development.

Johnston, J. H., and G. C. Markle. 1983. "What Research Says to the Practitioner about Ability Grouping." *Middle School Journal,* 14, 28–31.

Jones, M. G., and T. M. Gerig. 1994. "Ability Grouping and Classroom Interactions." *Journal of Classroom Interaction,* 29, 27–34.

Jongsma, K. S. 1990. "Collaborative Learning (Questions and Answers)." *The Reading Teacher,* 43, 346–347.

Juel, C. 1990. "The Effects of Reading Group Assignment on Reading Development in First and Second Grade." *Journal of Reading Behavior,* 22, 223–254.

Koskinen, P. S., and I. H. Blum. 1984. "Repeated Oral Reading and the Acquisition of Fluency." In *Changing Perspectives on Research in Reading/Language Processing Instruction: Thirty-Third Yearbook of the National Reading Conference*, edited by J. A. Niles and L. A. Harris. Rochester, NY: National Reading Conference.

————. 1986. "Paired Repeated Reading: A Classroom Strategy for Developing Fluent Reading." *The Reading Teacher*, 70, 70–75.

Kulik, C., and J. A. Kulik. 1982. "Effects of Ability Grouping on Secondary School Students: A Meta-analysis of Evaluation Findings." *American Educational Research Journal*, 19, 415–428.

Langer, J., A. Applebee, I. Mullis, and M. Foertsch. 1990. *Learning to Read in Our Nation's Schools: Instruction and Achievement in 1988 at Grades 4, 8, and 12.* Washington, DC: National Assessment of Educational Progress.

Leslie, L., and J. Caldwell. 2001. *The Qualitative Reading Inventory III.* New York: Addison Wesley Longman.

Limbrick, L., S. McNaughton, and M. Cameron. 1985. *Peer Power: Using Peer Tutoring to Help Low-progress Readers in Primary and Secondary Schools.* New Zealand Council for Educational Research.

Lou, Y., P. C. Abrami, and J. C. Spence. 2000. "Effects of Within-class Grouping on Student Achievement: An Exploratory Model." *Journal of Educational Research*, 94, 101–112.

Lou, Y., P. C. Abrami, J. C. Spence, C. Poulsen, B. Chambers, and S. d'Apollonia. 1996. "Within-class Grouping: A Meta-analysis." *Review of Educational Research*, 66, 423–458.

Lyman, F. 1988. "Think-pair-share." *MAACIE Cooperative News*, 2, 1.

MacKenzie, T., ed. 1992. *Readers' Workshop: Bridging Literature and Literacy.* New York: Irwin.

Madden, N. 1988. "Improving Reading Attitudes for Poor Readers through Cooperative Reading Teams." *The Reading Teacher*, 42, 194–199.

Madden, N., and R. E. Slavin. 1983. "Effects of Cooperative Learning on the Social Acceptance of Mainstreamed Academically Handicapped Students." *Journal of Special Education*, 17, 171–182.

Manarino-Leggett, P., and P. A. Salomon. 1989. *Cooperation or Competition: Techniques for Keeping Your Classroom Alive but not Endangered.* Paper read at the annual meeting of the International Reading Association, New Orleans, May 1989.

Marriott, D. 2002. *Comprehension Right from the Start: Book Clubs for Young Readers.* Portsmouth, NH: Heinemann.

Masland, S. 1990. "With Whole Class Reading Instruction, We're Not Out of the Woods Yet." *Wisconsin State Reading Association Journal,* 34, 31–35.

Mehan, H. 1979. *Learning Lessons: Social Organization in the Classroom.* Cambridge, MA: Harvard University Press.

Michigan Reading Association Studies and Research Committee. 1991. *Grouping Students for Literacy Learning: What Works.* Grand Rapids, MI: Michigan Reading Association.

Moody. S. W., S. Vaughn, and J. S. Schumm. 1997. "Instructional Grouping for Reading." *Remedial and Special Education,* 18, 347–356.

Nagel, G. 2000. *Effective Grouping for Literacy Instruction.* Boston: Allyn and Bacon.

Nystrand, M., and A. Gamoran. 1989. *Instructional Discourse and Student Engagement.* Paper prepared for the National Center for Effective Secondary Schools, Madison, WI.

Oakes, J. 1985. *Keeping Track: How Schools Structure Inequality.* New Haven, CT: Yale University Press.

———. 1988. "Tracking: Can Schools Take a Different Route?" *NEA Today, Issues '88,* 6, 41–47.

O'Donnell, M., and M. Wood. 1992. *Becoming a Reader: A Developmental Approach to Reading Instruction.* Boston: Allyn and Bacon.

Ogle, D. 1986. "K-W-L: A Teaching Model that Develops Active Reading of Expository Text." *The Reading Teacher,* 39, 564–570.

Ohlhausen, M., and M. Jepsen. 1992. "Lessons from Goldilocks: Someone's Been Choosing My Books, But I Can Make My Own Choices Now!" *The New Advocate,* 5, 31–46.

Opitz, M. F. 1992. "The Cooperative Reading Activity: An Alternative to Ability Grouping." *The Reading Teacher,* 45, 736–738.

Opitz, M., and M. Ford. 2001. *Reaching Readers: Flexible and Innovative Strategies for Guided Reading.* Portsmouth, NH: Heinemann.

Opitz, M., and T. Rasinski. 1999. *Say Goodbye to Round Robin Oral Reading.* Portsmouth. NH: Heinemann.

Palardy, J. M. 1991. "Public Elementary Schooling: Some Desirable Changes." *Reading Improvement,* 28, 149–152.

Palincsar, A. S., and A. L. Brown. 1984. "Reciprocal Teaching of Comprehension-fostering and Comprehension-monitoring Activities." *Cognition and Literacy,* 1, 117–175.

Paratore, J. 1990. *Classroom Contexts for Literacy Training: Flexible Grouping.* Paper read at the Wisconsin State Reading Association Fall Conference, 5–6 October, Eau Claire, WI.

Pearson, P. D., and M. C. Gallagher. 1983. "The Instruction of Reading Comprehension." *Contemporary Educational Psychology,* 8, 317–344.

Pflaum, S. W., E. T. Pascarella, M. Boswick, and C. Auer, 1980. "The Influence of Pupil Behaviors and Pupil Status Factors on Teacher Behaviors During Oral Reading Lessons." *Journal of Educational Research,* 74, 99–105.

Pilgreen, J. 2000. *The SSR Handbook: How to Organize and Manage a Sustained Silent Reading Program.* Portsmouth, NH: Heinemann.

Purvis, A. C. 1990. "Can Literature Be Rescued from Reading?" In *Transactions with Literature: A Fifty Year Perspective,* edited by E. Farrell and J. Squire. Urbana, IL: NCTE, 79–92.

Radencich, M. C., L. J. McKay, and J. R. Paratore. 1995. "Keeping Flexible Groups Flexible: Grouping Options." In *Flexible Grouping for Literacy in the Elementary Grades,* edited by M. C. Radencich and L. J. McKay. Boston: Allyn and Bacon, 25–41.

Raphael, T., and S. McMahon. 1997. *The Book Club Connection.* Newark, DE: The International Reading Association.

Rashotte, C. A., and J. K. Torgesen. 1985. "Repeated Reading and Reading Fluency in Learning Disabled Children." *Reading Research Quarterly,* 20, 180–188.

Reutzel, D. R. 1999. "Organizing Literacy Instruction: Effective Grouping Strategies and Organizational Plans." In *Best Practices in Literacy Instruction,* edited by L. B. Gambrell, L. M. Morrow, S. B. Neuman, and M. Pressley. New York: The Guilford Press, 271–290.

Reutzel, D. R., and R. B. Cooter, Jr. 1991. "Organizing for Effective Instruction: The Reading Workshop." *The Reading Teacher,* 44, 548–554.

———. 1996. *Teaching Children to Read: From Basals to Books.* Columbus, OH: Merrill, Prentice-Hall.

Riccio, L. L. 1985. "Facts and Issues about Ability Grouping." *Contemporary Education*, 57, 26–30.

Richek, M. A. 1987. "DR-TA: 5 Variations that Facilitate Independence in Reading Narratives." *Journal of Reading*, 40, 632–636.

Richek, M. A., J. S. Caldwell, J. H. Jennings, and J. W. Lerner. 2002. *Reading Problems: Assessment and Teaching Strategies.* Boston: Allyn and Bacon.

Routman, R. 1999. *Conversations: Strategies for Teaching, Learning and Evaluating.* Portsmouth, NH: Heinemann.

Rowan, B., and A. W. Miracle, Jr. 1983. "Systems of Ability Grouping and the Stratification of Achievement in Elementary Schools: A Best-evidence Synthesis." *Sociology of Education*, 56, 133–144.

Samuels, S. J. 1979. "The Method of Repeated Reading." *The Reading Teacher*, 32, 403–408.

Serafini, F. 2001. *The Reading Workshop: Making Space for Readers.* Portsmouth, NH: Heinemann.

Sharpley, A. M., and C. F. Sharpley. 1981. "Peer Tutoring—A Review of the Literature." *Collected Original Resources in Education*, 5, 7–112.

Slavin, R. E. 1982. "Cooperative Learning: Student Teams." *What Research Says to the Teacher.* Washington, DC: National Education Association.

———. 1983. *Student Team Learning.* Washington, DC: National Education Association.

———. 1987. "Ability Grouping and Student Achievement in Elementary Schools: A Best-evidence Synthesis." *Review of Educational Research*, 57, 293–336.

———. 1988. "Cooperative Learning and Student Achievement." *Educational Leadership*, 45, 31–33.

———. 1990. "Achievement Effects of Ability Grouping in Secondary Schools: A Best-evidence Synthesis." *Review of Educational Research*, 60, 471–499.

———. 1991. "Are Cooperative Learning and 'Untracking' Harmful to the Gifted?" *Educational Leadership*, 48, 68–71.

Slavin, R. E., and N. Karweit. 1981. "Cognitive and Affective Outcomes of an Intensive Student Team Learning Experience." *Journal of Experimental Education*, 50, 29–35.

Smith, F. 1988. *Understanding Reading.* Hillsdale, NJ: Erlbaum.

Sorenson, A. B., and M. Hallinan, 1986. "Effects of Ability Grouping on Growth in Academic Achievement." *American Educational Research Journal,* 23, 519–542.

Stahl, S. A., and K. Heubach. 1993. *Changing Reading Instruction in Second Grade: A Fluency-oriented Reading Program.* Paper read at the National Reading Conference. Charleston, SC, December 1993.

Stallings, J. A., and D. Stipek. 1985. "Research on Early Childhood and Elementary School Teaching Programs." In *Handbook on Research on Teaching,* edited by M. C. Wittrock. New York: Macmillan, 727–753.

Stevens, R. J., N. A. Madden, R. E. Slavin, and A. M. Farnish. 1987. "Cooperative Integrated Reading and Composition: Two Field Experiments." *Reading Research Quarterly,* 22, 433–454.

Strike, K. A. 1983. "Fairness and Ability Grouping." *Educational Theory,* 33, 125–134.

Topping K. 1987. "Paired Reading: A Powerful Technique for Parent Use." *The Reading Teacher,* 40, 604–614.

———. 1988. *The Peer Tutoring Handbook: Promoting Cooperative Learning.* Cambridge, MA: Brookline.

———. 1989. "Peer Tutoring and Paired Reading: Combining Two Powerful Techniques." *The Reading Teacher,* 42, 488–494.

Uttero, D. A. 1988. "Activating Comprehension through Cooperative Learning." *The Reading Teacher,* 41, 390–395.

Wade, S. E., and E. B. Moje. 2000. "The Role of Text in Classroom Learning." In *Handbook of Reading Research, Vol. III,* edited by M. L. Kamil, P. B. Mosenthal, P. D. Pearson, and R. Barr. New York: Erlbaum, 609–628.

Weinstein, R. S. 1976. "Reading Group Membership in First Grade: Teacher Behaviors and Pupil Experience Over Time." *Journal of Educational Psychology,* 68, 103–116.

Wilkinson, I. A. G., and M. A. R. Townsend. 2000. "From Rata to Rimu: Grouping for Instruction in Best Practice New Zealand Classrooms." *The Reading Teacher,* 53, 460–471.

Wood. K. D. 1987. "Fostering Cooperative Learning in Middle and Secondary Level Classrooms." *Journal of Reading*, 30, 10–18.

Worthy, J., K. Broaddus, and G. Ivey. 2001. *Pathways to Independence: Reading, Writing and Learning in Grades 3–8*. New York: Guilford.

Young, T. A., and D. McCullough. 1992. "Looking Out for Low-achieving Readers." *Reading Horizons*, 32, 394–402.